IF YOU'VE ENCOUNTERED ANY
OF THESE PROBLEMS—

She can't stand it when I give her advice. . . . Why does he always invalidate my feelings? . . . I have to walk on eggshells when I talk to her. . . . How do I know if someone I'm attracted to is attracted too? . . . I'm uncomfortable talking to an audience of the opposite sex.

IT'S TIME YOU SOLVED IT

Written in a humorous and personal voice, this valuable guide to communicating with the opposite sex gives you down-to-earth advice on sending and receiving messages effectively. You'll learn how to avoid the pitfalls posed by the differences in gender-speak.

FIND OUT ABOUT

- Do's and don'ts for better conversations with your mate
- Strategies for dealing with anger, at home or at work
- The non-nagger's success manual
- A primer for comforting someone of the opposite sex
- How to give criticism without giving offense
- The secrets of "tantalizing listening"—really turning him or her on with the way you tune in
- And much more . . .

LAURIE SCHLOFF is director of executive training at The Speech Improvement Company in Boston, Massachusetts. She provides communication coaching to individuals and groups.
MARCIA YUDKIN, a freelance writer and consultant, is also based in Boston. Laurie Schloff and Marcia Yudkin are the co-authors of *Smart Speaking* (Plume).

Also by Laurie Schloff and Marcia Yudkin

SMART SPEAKING

Laurie Schloff and
Marcia Yudkin

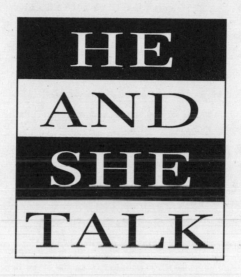

HE
AND
SHE
TALK

How to Communicate
with the Opposite Sex

A PLUME BOOK

PLUME
Published by the Penguin Group
Penguin Books USA Inc., 375 Hudson Street,
New York, New York 10014, U.S.A.
Penguin Books Ltd, 27 Wrights Lane, London W8 5TZ, England
Penguin Books Australia Ltd, Ringwood, Victoria, Australia
Penguin Books Canada Ltd, 10 Alcorn Avenue,
Toronto, Ontario, Canada M4V 3B2
Penguin Books (N.Z.) Ltd, 182–190 Wairau Road,
Auckland 10, New Zealand

Penguin Books Ltd, Registered Offices:, Harmondsworth, Middlesex, England

First published by Plume, an imprint of New American Library,
a division of Penguin Books USA Inc.

First Printing, August, 1993

10 9 8 7 6 5 4 3 2 1

 REGISTERED TRADEMARK—MARCA REGISTRADA

LIBRARY OF CONGRESS CATALOGING-IN-PUBLICATION DATA
Schloff, Laurie.
    He and she talk : how to communicate with the opposite sex / Laurie
Schloff and Marcia Yudkin.
        p.   cm.
    ISBN 0-452-27066-9
    1. Interpersonal communication.   2. Sex differences (Psychology)
3. Man-woman relationships.   I. Yudkin, Marcia.   II. Title.
BF637.C45S355   1993
155.3'3—dc20   92-45217
                                                                          CIP

Printed in the United States of America
Designed by Eve L. Kirch

BOOKS ARE AVAILABLE AT QUANTITY DISCOUNTS WHEN USED TO PROMOTE
PRODUCTS OR SERVICES. FOR INFORMATION PLEASE WRITE TO PREMIUM
MARKETING DIVISION, PENGUIN BOOKS USA INC., 375 HUDSON STREET, NEW
YORK, NEW YORK 10014.

CONTENTS

FRIENDS, DATES, AND FAMILY

PROFESSIONALLY SPEAKING

PREFACE

The Golden Rule may well be the most widely known combination of eleven words in the English language: "Do unto others as you would have them do unto you." Unfortunately, where communication between the sexes is concerned, this revered principle steers us more in the direction of conflict and misunderstanding than toward harmony and rapport. It's now well-established that on the whole, men and women differ in communication habits, expectations, and preferences. When we communicate with the opposite sex the way we like others to communicate with us—as most of us instinctively do—we're often setting the stage for misinterpretation and frustration. This book provides practical, situational advice and specific strategies that produce more satisfying results, even when only one communication partner uses them. We offer sensible solutions for common difficulties in getting through at home, at work, and with friends, dates, and relatives.

Wherever possible, we've briefly indicated data from studies and surveys that delineate gender differences in communication. We see most of these differences as stemming not from genes or hormones but from divergent ways in which males and females are encouraged to behave as children and rewarded as adults. As you read, please remember that no generalization or pattern implied in this book applies 100 percent. We've tried to implement our awareness that statistics may not match all situations by alternating male and female names and pronouns within chapters and occasionally featuring examples that turn popular stereotypes upside down.

We differ from some other authors on male-female communication in assuming that awareness of gender differences in communication is just the first step toward more productive, constructive relationships. When both sides are motivated to improve communication, you can discuss changes each of you feels comfortable with that reduce the stress of miscommunication and increase the chances of mutual understanding. When your communication partner isn't motivated to change, you still have three options in trying to resolve the problem: you can decide simply to accept your differences, you can change your behavior to adapt to the other person, or you can try to influence the other person to alter his or her mode of communication. Remember that you don't have the power to change another person's behavior or attitudes. But by changing how you act, react, and think around the other person, you can set in motion more satisfying communication dynamics.

Feel free to start reading this book anywhere and to skip around among the chapters that are most applicable to your current communication problems. We've sometimes included cross-references to chapters that provide related information and advice.

This is a practical book, and you'll often need some practice before you notice results. When you try a new communication technique, such as arguing back where you used to sulk or asking questions where you used to dictate solutions, you may not immediately feel comfortable with your changed behavior. Keep trying anyway, since repetition makes new behavior familiar and your strategy may have a delayed or cumulative impact. Give each technique ten tries before giving it up or concluding that it doesn't work.

We'd like to thank Diana Finch, our literary agent, and Deborah Brody, our editor, for assisting in the birth of this book, as well as the men's groups in Belmont and Salem, Massachusetts, which shared insights and suggestions with us. In addition, Marcia thanks Liz Curtis Higgs and Patti Wood for information on male-female differences in communication and Gila, Joan, and Florence Yudkin for feedback, ideas, and encouragement. Laurie thanks Gertrude Schloff for her support and frequent correspondence and Dennis and Paula Becker at The Speech Improvement Company for outstanding daily collegial communication. To Laurie's husband, Ed Horowitz, thanks for being "someone to love"—and now, please read this book!

We'd love to hear stories of what worked and didn't, as well as suggestions for topics in our future books on productive communication. Write to Laurie Schloff at The Speech Improvement Company, 1614 Beacon St., Brookline, MA 02146 (617-739-3330) or to Marcia Yudkin at P.O. Box 1310, Boston, MA 02117.

COUPLES
COMMUNICATION

My partner says I'm insensitive, but I don't agree.

What you view as sensitive behavior and what she views as sensitive behavior may not match. Althea wanted Joe to ask how she was feeling every day, not an easy task for Joe, who rarely stopped to think how *he* was feeling. Joe thought he showed sensitivity by taking off Althea's shoes and tucking her in when she fell asleep reading at night. Althea didn't seem to appreciate the small things he did for her all the time. To her, only talking counted.

With sensitivity, you understand another's perspective and then through words or actions manifest that understanding. For example, your fiancée is shy, so even though *you'd* like a big birthday bash, you won't be throwing a big surprise party for her thirtieth. Gender differences in upbringing steer the sexes differently when it comes to showing sensitivity. By adulthood, women are more skilled than men in conveying empathy through listening, accepting, agreeing, and adopting compassionate facial expressions and eye contact. When a woman doesn't receive these responses from the man in her life, she may label him insensitive. Men, accustomed to showing feelings through action rather than describing them verbally, may consider *their* partners insensitive for not appreciating well-intended opinions, the favors they do, and their giving up a night out with the guys to stay home together.

Since the gift of understanding is one of the most precious you could ever give in a relationship, consider spending some time on—

Sensitivity training, updated for the nineties

1. *Consciousness raising*. Wake up to the notion that you two differ on what constitutes sensitive behavior. Complete this checklist and have your partner do so as well.

Sensitivity checklist

Check which behaviors signal "sensitive" to you.

_____ attention to what I'm saying
_____ affirmation that my views make sense
_____ appreciation of how I naturally show interest and concern
_____ listening without giving an opinion
_____ listening and offering advice, agreement, or disagreement
_____ noticing what I've achieved
_____ asking about my day before and after
_____ surprising me with gifts, cards, notes, etc.
_____ being left alone
_____ pushing me to better myself
_____ complimenting
_____ offering constructive criticism
_____ avoiding any kind of criticism
_____ showering me with affection and physical attention
_____ avoiding painful or sore subjects

4

_____ talking out problems
_____ doing favors without asking
_____ understanding my good and bad sides
_____ not expecting more than I can give at the
moment
_____ being comfortable with quiet times
_____ asking my feelings about people and events
_____ not probing my feelings too much
_____ other _____

2. *Tune in, turn on.* Once you know what makes your loved one's sensitivity sensors tingle, resolve to add one or two behaviors on her list to your repertoire. Joe chucked the tucking in for tuning in to Althea's everyday feelings. Though he couldn't really understand the value of a simple question like "How did you feel about that?" Althea was thrilled with his efforts to show interest.

3. *Or drop out.* If you'd feel too unnatural doing what your partner designates as sensitive, say so. At least she'll know it's not insensitivity holding you back.
"Althea, it's just not in me to compliment you *every* time we get dressed to go out."

I talk more easily with friends than with my partner.

For many, the ideal is a mate who they can truthfully say is their best friend. However, people choose lifelong lovers for reasons besides conversational compatibility. Loving may be more linked with lust, mutual life goals, or day-to-day comfort than deep discourse. One client whose recently laid-off wife now had time to meet him daily at noon bemoaned this new opportunity to be bored together. "I married her for life, but not for lunch," he said.

Recently researchers in the Department of Communication Studies at the University of Iowa asked 1,585 people to observe and rate their satisfaction with everyday conversations. Overall, those in the study rated conversational quality with lovers as less satisfying than interactions with relatives, best friends, and friends. (A couple of other curious findings: Conflicts in conversation occurred most on Wednesdays, and interacting with females on a regular basis correlated with better health.)

My client Ruth told me that whereas communication with her husband Christopher used to be tense, now they were on the best keel they'd had since their honeymoon. Hoping for an insight that would help others, I asked what had changed. She replied breezily, "Oh, we just don't talk to each other that much any more." Apparently Ruth had made peace with the reality that mates may never be your best conversational partners.

Do's and don'ts for dealing with conversational letdown.

Do acknowledge that some of your conversational needs are best met elsewhere. Ruth gets much satisfaction

6

discussing her struggles with self-esteem and her problems getting along with the other members of her car pool with her best friend Kathy.

Don't expect your mate to meet all your conversational needs. Stop dreaming that somehow he'll change. Ruth's emotional equilibrium comes from accepting that she did not marry the ideal communicator. Instead, she focuses on the more satisfying parts of their relationship—their common interest in hockey and watching old movies.

Do understand the factors which affect the quality of your conversation. The study mentioned above had participants rate conversations along these dimensions:

relaxed	strained
impersonal	personal
attentive	poor listener
formal	informal
in-depth	superficial
smooth	difficult
guarded	open
much understanding	much misunderstanding
no communication breakdowns	many communication breakdowns
free of conflict	laden with conflict
interesting	boring

To rate your conversations, put an "X" at the appropriate point along the spectrum between the extremes. If you rate conversations with your mate for these factors for a week, you should get a handle on how you talk with each other.

Don't give up. If you want your relationship to continue, mediocre conversations are healthier than none.

Once you know your patterns, strategize some ways to upgrade your conversational quality. Though Ruth would have preferred deep discussions, she knew what to expect with concrete Chris. Instead, interchanges about mundane daily details of life, like their broken dishwasher, provided the conversational contact important for a couple.

My partner doesn't listen.

In 1987, Shere Hite asked 4,000 American women, "What does your partner do that makes you the maddest?" A whopping 77 percent responded, "He doesn't listen." Gender differences in the hows and whys of tuning in add to the conflict over this vital component of communication.

Lynn remembers the early years when Claude hung on her every word. Eight years later, she wonders if some weird listening disability has afflicted her husband. Claude can't focus on more than ten words of hers before picking up the newspaper or a stereo magazine. While turning pages, he'll offer an appeasing "oh yeah" or "that's nice." When she accuses him of not listening, he protests that he knows every word she said and proves it by repeating her story verbatim. For his part, Claude describes dinner with Lynn as a demanding experience. After eight hours of accounting, he feels like spacing out, but she wants his undivided attention. "Plus," he adds, "she always asks for my opinion about work or the kids. She'll act like she's agreeing and then do nothing at all about it."

Claude and Lynn, and millions of couples everywhere, are missing out on the most provocative gift you can give a significant other—tantalizing listening.

Men: How to make her go wild when you listen

1. *Look into her eyes.*

2. *Put no barriers between the two of you* (newspapers, VCRs, *Consumer Reports*, short-wave radios).

3. *Make sounds that will turn her on.* Try zesty *mmhmms*, *uh huhs*, and *really?*s when she pauses. These

9

signal that you want more. Most men hold back and sound uninterested, but women like a lot of reinforcement during the act of talking.

4. *Do it with your whole body*. Lean in, nod, use lots of facial expression—don't stop. Focus on her pleasure.

5. *Stay centered on her rhythm*. Don't quickly switch to your needs. To overwhelm her, agree with something she said. Breathe deeply—you can handle the buildup.

6. *Go all the way*. If you've earnestly done all the above, you can be sure she'll want to give you her all. Try bringing up your own subject and notice how eagerly she yields to you now.

Women: How to make him go wild when you listen (You probably tune in well, but do you turn him on?)

1. *Be feisty*. Jump into his rap with your own opinions. Even dare to interrupt. Don't let him exhaust himself in a monologue.

2. *Don't tease*. Stop playing along as if you really want his advice or opinion without following through. Guys take your nods and avid interest seriously. If you find your head bobbing and your voice uh-huhing even though you don't agree, play fair and tell him your reservations.

3. *Play it cool*. Women give so many listening signals—great eye contact, eyebrow lifts and smiles, ques-

10

tioning him as if he's on "Sixty Minutes"—that he may find the situation overwhelming. Tone down on tuning in and he'll be longing for your interchange.

> Your most important sex organs are your ears. Use them shrewdly.

She complains I don't like to talk — and I don't.

Women have the reputation for being the gabbier sex. Research indicates, though, that talkativeness is not gender related but situational. For example, in mixed-sex groups in social and work situations, men speak more often and speak longer when they have the floor. At home with each other, however, women and men may have very different ideas about the importance of talking. Women commonly want to relate, and assume an intimate relationship requires conversation. Men frequently prefer to relax, and feel that being together without talking expresses intimacy. The result is that men may feel pressured to talk "against their will" and resent having to make the effort. Sometimes the more she talks, the less he responds. When she's delivering monologues and he's dispensing an occasional grunt, it's time for a couple to communicate about communicating.

When your minimum daily conversation requirements differ—

1. *Be clear.* When you're not in the mood to talk, you can be direct and tactful. This beats making supposedly meaningful noises when you're really concentrating on the sports pages. (Guess what, guys—women know when you've left Planet Earth, so you might as well admit it.) State your feeling without blaming.

"I don't feel like talking right now."

"I can't really concentrate on what you're saying."

"I need quiet for a while."

12

2. *Be a dear*. Give her a break. If you value your relationship, compromise on a way for you to participate in regular conversation. Arrange a time, set some limits, or make a date to talk.

"Let's discuss it after the news."

"Can we set aside fifteen minutes at breakfast tomorrow to discuss getting our money back from that plumber?"

"Let's talk about our vacation plans Wednesday after dinner. My grant proposal will be finished then."

3. *Be surprised!* Conversational disinterest may be a way you avoid getting too close or just a bad habit you picked up from Dad. Don't faint, but it's possible over time that you'll enjoy more talking time together.

Nate and Trudy agreed to touch base at bedtime, the one chance they always had to see each other. At first Nate wanted to sack out when Trudy began to share details of her day. But before long, Nate was the one spilling out his work woes and trying to keep his bedmate awake at the same time.

I'm always more interested in talking than he is.

Welcome to the one-way conversation club. Though plenty of men turn somersaults to get conversational action going with their mates, more often women end up exasperated with silent partners. It's not that women bore men—watch a man salivate over her every syllable on a long-awaited first date. Rather, whereas women tend to need a daily dose of conversational closeness, men value just being together and doing things together, even mundane activities like eating quietly side by side. For guys, verbal interaction is one part, and not necessarily the most important part, of the whole relationship picture. This frustrates women who judge closeness by the number of words exchanged per evening. If wives and girlfriends had their druthers, the time couples spend in conversation would surely rise from its measly weekly average of nineteen—yes, nineteen—minutes.

To defuse conversational frustration—

1. *Don't let it get to you.* In a fundamentally sound relationship, conversational reluctance doesn't mean rejection. Recognize that for you conversation is a form of coupling, while for him talk may be just words.

2. *Stop taking the initiative in verbal interactions.* Change your conversational patterns and watch what happens. If you're generally the driving force for dinner talk, try holding back. There's a fifty-fifty chance that silence will stimulate your taciturn partner's vocal cords. Maura seemed to stump husband Cal with the question, "How was your day?" which she asked every night like clockwork

while they were lounging around before dinner. Three days into Maura's assignment of not prompting conversation, Cal did a surprising thing. He said, "Don't you care about how my day went?" Managing to restrain her eagerness to hear, Maura responded casually, "Oh yes, how was it?" He talked about ten times longer than his usual "All right" or "Nothing special."

3. *Bring up the subject of your conversational needs*. When both you and he are in a decent mood, be direct without blaming. Let your partner know what's important to you.

"I know you like a lot of quiet. I need to talk every day to touch base and feel close."

4. *Once you have discussed your different needs, explore some middle ground*. For example, set up a regular talking time. Nothing formal, just a time like dinner or before bedtime that you agree to devote to catching up with each other for five or ten minutes. You'll know the connecting time is coming, and he'll know it will end at some point. Not conversational heaven but a good couples compromise.

5. *Don't be conversationally monogamous*. Having other people in your life to chat with besides your mate lessens the pressure on both of you. When Maura came home dying to complain about her boss and found Cal engulfed in a video game, she learned to call up her chum Kathryn instead.

6. *If all else fails, talk to yourself*. Self-gratification can be a great tension release.

She complains I don't like to talk about feelings.

Women's preference for talk about relationships, people, and feelings contrasts sharply with many men's preference for less personal topics such as business, politics, and sports. Interestingly, despite the fact that many women have joined male-dominated fields, topic preferences in conversation haven't changed much since the early part of the century. One 1920s' researcher with an interesting laboratory—Broadway—eavesdropped on passersby. He found that half of the man-to-man conversations centered on money and business, while only 3 percent of the woman-to-woman conversations did. And where almost half of the woman-woman talk concerned men, only 8 percent of the men were discussing women with each other. In 1989, another eavesdropping researcher studied casual conversations among bank officers at lunch. She found that women conversing with women talked most about relationships and second most about business. Among the men, business talk predominated and they never talked about people.

Although men tend to find feelings talk as foreign a language as French, some effort to *parlez* emotions will narrow the gender gap. You'll probably find, as women have for centuries, that feelings talk feels good and deepens friendship and intimacy. Don't worry, men, you will not turn into mush. There is football after feelings.

Tactics for feelings talk

1. *Expect to fumble*. Talking about unexplored territory can feel awkward. Don't let that stop you.

2. *Keep the goal in mind*. You talk about feelings not to impress, prove, or persuade. The goal of this game is being genuine. You even score points for admitting a vulnerability. Women see sharing a weakness as a sign of trust.

3. *Punt*. Take small steps. You don't have to wail about your traumatic toilet training. Disclose your feelings about the new phone system in the office.

"I'm worried that Marge will never learn how to operate all those new phone features."

4. *Learn the lingo*. Your partner probably has years more practice with terminology in the realm of feelings. Get into the game by reviewing the basic vocabulary. Get into shape by using one or two items from this list every day.

The top twenty feeling words

"I feel or I am . . ."

> ambivalent
> angry
> annoyed
> concerned
> confident
> confused
> embarrassed
> exhausted
> freaking out
> furious
> happy
> insecure

nervous
overwhelmed
pressured
sad
scared
surprised
uncomfortable
worried

5. *You can drop out of the game.* Feelings talk includes the right not to express feelings. Just say so.

"I don't feel comfortable talking about my divorce yet."

"I'm not ready to deal with discussing our taxes. I'm still too upset."

He invalidates my feelings.

We all yearn to feel understood and accepted in communication. Research in the field of counseling has shown that the more personal the situation or feeling expressed, the stronger our desire for an empathic "I know what you mean" response. When someone to whom we confess intimate matters puts down, diminishes, or discredits what we say, we feel disappointed, alienated, or even violated. Since more women than men play the understanding role in relationships, and men verbalize feelings less often than women, we can guess that more females than males feel that their mates "just don't get it." Men more often feel invalidated when their partner doesn't appreciate their perspective on the world, or the intention behind their behavior, or when mates don't accept them for who they are. It's vital to recognize that some people rarely tune into their own feelings, never mind yours. If he gives himself an "oh grow up" lecture when he's hurting, he'll find it difficult to be a source of comfort when you need one.

Clancy, an electronics wizard, would hear the slightest hum from his sound system and know exactly what wire needed readjustment. He was less attuned to his fiancée, Fran. She found Clancy's lectures to forget her unhappy childhood and "move on with her life" exasperating. In sharing a poignant memory, Fran didn't feel she was dwelling on the past, just seeing it more clearly. Fran wished there was some way to get through to Clancy how much she wanted to be simply heard and confirmed.

Options when you're emotionally evicted

1. *Be your own counsel*. If your partner is prone to a punitive reaction, don't aid and abet this tendency. Keep feelings separate and share them with more respectful listeners. (Hopefully, your mate has strong points that compensate.)

2. *Issue a summons*. In direct terms, say what you need. Most likely her crimes aren't motivated by malice but by mismatched perspectives. Examples of how to share your need:
"I have the right to feel the way I feel."
"I can't stand it when you tell me my feelings are wrong or stupid."
"It's my life and I can cry if I want to."
"F—— off, Clancy, that's the way I feel!"

3. *Put him on probation*. Give him a chance to rehabilitate his reactions. Try this three-step program:
First, educate. Describe the differences between the way you two handle feelings.
"I don't mind crying, but you do. My feelings are important to me, and it hurts when you make fun of me for having them."
Second, look for signs of progress and reward them.
"I appreciated it when you didn't try to talk me out of being mad."
Third, don't tempt him. Sidestep the pattern by presenting your thoughts without the emotional words that might provoke him. For example:

DON'T SAY: "I am nauseated by the way that woman flirted with you."
TO WHICH HE'D SAY: "Don't get so worked up."
TRY: "I noticed that that woman got real close to you."

DON'T SAY: "I'm really freaked out about the presentation to the board of trustees tomorrow."

TO WHICH HE'D SAY: "Why? You've done it a million times before."

BETTER: "My presentation to the board of trustees tomorrow is really important. I have to do a good job."

A *proposed Freedom of Feelings Amendment*

Given that human beings feel feelings; that feelings do not harm others or society; and that feelings can only be changed or controlled by the feeler; each party in a relationship is therefore entitled to freely express feelings without undue interference or hostility.

21

She turns the most ordinary conversations into a conflict.

Jerry found it impossible to have a relaxing conversation with Liz. A topic as banal as bananas became fodder for her combative nitpicking. He gave this example of their less than fruitful interaction.

The Banana Incident: Take One

Jerry: These bananas are a real steal, only thirty cents a pound.
Liz: Well, they're probably rotten.
Jerry: They look good to me.
Liz: So now you're a banana expert too.

Jerry couldn't understand why Liz went out of her way to create clashes, since they both had plenty of it in their investment-banking jobs. He thought people in a relationship ought to try to be agreeable, or at least pick battles over things bigger than a bunch of bananas. Usually the peacemaker, Jerry was starting to go bananas over what he described as Liz's constant verbal lashing.

Rather than a sign that Liz didn't want to get along, her contentious conversation reflected her communicative style. Jerry and Liz's pattern occurs commonly with the man more adversarial and the woman more accommodating. Surprisingly, those with a testy tendency view their behavior as a sign that they care and want the best for their partner (Liz said she didn't want Jerry to be fooled by a low price when other considerations were also relevant in banana buying). Duelers find the rivalry exhilarating and miss it when the other half of their duo doesn't spar back. Jerry and other serenity-seeking spouses thrive on mutual stroking and find Liz's style exhausting. Jerry may have been seeing Liz in the wrong light, but he still needed to learn—

How to live with a lion

1. *Tame him with caution*. Your opposite may not realize how he comes across or how he affects you. Men who use verbal boxing as a way of bonding, for example, may find it hard to understand that their true intentions aren't clear as a kiss. Give specific examples of what bugs you and what could be a less combative way of putting things. Although he may not change, you've at least identified your differences.

"I notice that when I say black, you say white. Just now all I said was that these bananas look good, and you had to put down my opinion. How about if you just said nothing or didn't make a big deal over a bunch of bananas?"

2. *Go ahead and growl back*. You hold a belief that closeness comes from consensus, not banter. Not necessarily! Try giving it back to build up your growling stamina. Don't go overboard, though. Think Hepburn and Tracy, not *The War of the Roses*.

The Banana Incident: Take Two

Jerry: These bananas are a real steal, only thirty cents a pound.
Liz: Well, they're probably rotten.
Jerry: Cool it, you didn't even look at them.
Liz: Yeah, so since when are you a banana expert?
Jerry: Excuse me, I didn't know you had a Ph.D. in fruit inspection.

23

He or she wants me to confide everything.

Arthur told me that Rochelle, his woman friend of ten years, felt they should not have any secrets. "If she had her way, we'd be one huge glob," he put it. "I like more boundaries." To Rochelle and some other mates, willingness to tell all indicates trust. To others, unlimited confessions grate against their sense of privacy. Many girls grow up cementing friendships by sharing secrets. The deeper the secret, the tighter the connection. As adults, a no-secrets stance consequently comes more naturally to many women. Pair up these two types and you get a tug of war about sharing information. The more intimacy expected, the more he feels invaded, while the less openness offered, the less she feels bonded.

How to handle colliding about confiding

1. *Be discreet about your private affairs*. Remember that to your mate sharing secrets denotes solidarity, not surrender. Don't make a big deal about the things you keep to yourself. For example:

DON'T SAY: "You'll never know anything about my insecurities."
TRY: "You're much better at talking about yourself than I am."

DON'T SAY: "I am not going to tell you about the ins and outs of promotions at my law firm."
TRY: "I'm never really sure what's happening at work with promotions. Things change so quickly all the time."

2. *Consider the option of opening up.* You always have the right not to reveal. Still, think about what you may have to gain by breaking through your own privacy barriers. Try to weigh these privacy pros and cons:

Good reasons for staying closed

- You don't trust him to keep the information private.
- You're concerned about her emotional reaction.
- You're protecting someone else's privacy.
- You need time to mull over the information.

Good reasons for revealing yourself more

- You would feel better for telling him.
- You could benefit from her input or feedback.
- You can't think of one benefit of being closed.

Arthur decided that while he wanted to keep Rochelle in the dark about the nasty infighting at the office, talking about his parents' age-seventy divorce would help him feel less burdened on this sad topic. To his surprise, she responded by saying she now understood more why he was so skittish about marriage. "Hmm," he said to himself, "I wonder if that *is* the reason."

3. *Draw explicit boundary lines.* If your significant other oversteps your boundaries to the point where the push and pull perturbs both of you, bring up the issue directly. You want to hold your ground without making her feel as if the foundation between the two of you is faltering.

State differences in your beliefs about the right to

privacy. "You want to share everything. I'm not like that. I prefer to keep some things about my past to myself."

Then state how you'd like her to relate to you. "So if I don't want to talk about my past romances, I don't want you to push me."

I don't want my partner talking about me with her friends.

Jeanne attributed her survival as a mother of triplet toddlers to the support she received in her weekly mothers' group. Carlos, her husband, supported her involvement in the support group—until the mothers started talking about money and sexual problems. When Carlos told Jeanne to leave the deep stuff at home, Jeanne became weepy. "I'll go nuts if I can't tell them what's really going on!"

Like many men, Carlos would never have chosen to share vulnerabilities with *his* friends, not to mention hers. From his point of view, talking about him behind his back constituted a serious betrayal. Yet like many women, Jeanne felt that the foundation of friendship is exchange about the intimate details of life. Carlos and Jeanne needed to strike a balance between his right to privacy and her right to confide in friends. Since confusion about basic rights and wrongs abounds here, creating an explicit pact may help.

Privacy Pact for Partners

For the private partner:

- I agree to let my partner know what I don't want her friends to know. I cannot assume she'll read my mind on this. "I'd prefer it if you didn't talk about my prostate problem to Dora."
- I understand that my partner is not motivated by malice but by a desire to get support, advice, etc.

from friends. Though I don't share this need, I can appreciate this difference.

- I understand that in the course of her conversation with friends, my name is bound to come up. Since she cares about me, I trust that she can restrain herself when revelations would cause me discomfort.

- I can ease up a bit. If Gail knows I'm a lazy lover or negligent about the lawn, will it really affect my life?

For the revealer:

- I have a responsibility to guard my partner's privacy regarding conversational topics. If he requests that I refrain from discussing something involving him, I must. It is OK to say, "I can't really talk about our money situation," or "Fred doesn't want me to go into detail about his learning disability."
- I have the right to discuss anything about me with close friends.
- I will try to focus conversations with friends on my needs, reactions, and issues, not his.

Your partner has a right to privacy—don't infringe on it.

She likes to analyze everything in our relationship/I prefer to let things be.

Frank loved the spontaneity of the early days of his relationship with April, but as their feelings grew more serious, so did she. Frank felt as dissected as the biology-class frog when April constantly questioned his behavior and motives. "Why do you want us to go out with your friends? You never used to." "How come we never get together on Friday nights?" "Why don't you call your mother more often?" When April subjected him to the third degree about his love for her with "How do you know it's love? What makes you sure it's the real thing?" Frank felt hurt and frustrated. "Can't we just enjoy the relationship and stop analyzing it?" he pleaded.

Though analyzing a relationship may prove great fun for a couple of therapists, many partners find such heady questioning aggravating. Like April, women may have more of a desire to dissect, because they thrive on talking about relationships and find it a way to get to know a partner better. Yet men frequently question the motives of an investigative reporter mate, saying that they feel cornered by the questions. They claim that the inquiries are loaded and that she's out to find a flaw and recommend changes. Frank fumed when April asked him to justify actions and feelings—he wanted her to accept him as he was. She said delving was just her style, not a way to do him in. Here are some suggestions for Frank and other folks who get uncomfortable:

When relationships are analyzed to the nth degree—

1. *Appreciate where she's coming from.* Try to distinguish a probe that resembles a cattle prod from a question of curiosity or concern. The phrasing of a prod makes you feel that no matter how you respond, you'll land in a trap.

- Prods: "Frank, how come you put everyone but me first when you make plans for Friday night?"
"Why do you ignore your mother on holidays?"

- Reasonable questions: "How come we don't get together on Fridays?"
"Does it upset your mother when you don't call her on holidays?"

If you decide that a reasonable question deserves a reasonable response, read on.

2. *If it feels right, respond.* You have several options.

- Let it all hang out. If you feel it's worthwhile to discuss the matter, go for it. A positively probing partner often listens sensitively too. For starters, use these opening phrases:

"Maybe it's because . . ."
"I never thought about it, but . . ."
"Now that you bring that up . . ."
"Ever since my . . ."

- Wait till I'm on the couch. Tell her to hang on for a better time and place.
"I need to concentrate in this traffic. Can we talk about my mother some night between reruns on the TV?"

"April, this was supposed to be a romantic moment. Can we save figuring out our relationship till later?"

• It's not my problem. With this response, you acknowledge his curiosity while indicating that you'd rather not discuss the subject.

"I know you're interested in my family dynamics, but I don't remember the past much and prefer not to go into it."

"I can see that you like to talk about these things, but as far as I'm concerned, I know what I feel, and that's that."

And, advice for the analytical (Getting deep without getting into deep trouble)

1. *Pick your picky points.* If your partner is not a prober, more than one "why?" question an evening will be exhausting to her.

2. *Don't play mind games.* Your partner needs acceptance from you, not amateur psychoanalysis. Don't camouflage your own hangups in questions about his psychology. Before you ask what gives in his relationship with Mom, think, "How will anyone benefit from figuring this out?" Also, if you do ask a question, don't scold when you receive a truthful answer. ("I can't stand my mother. That's why I didn't send a birthday card.")

3. *Avoid "whys."* The word "why" elicits a defensive reaction in many. Instead phrase questions with gentler starters like "How come," "What do you think about," "How did you react to," or "What's your impression of."

31

4. *Tell him your dreams.* If you really want your mate to make analytical conversation back, explain in appealing terms why you want to know. Present the benefit of his going into the matter.

"Frank, I'd like to get closer to your mother. So I'd like to hear why you think she's hard to relate to."

She likes to talk problems to death.

Robert wishes a weekend would go by without Myra going on and on about her frustrated artistic ambitions. She's ignored his advice and still expects him to listen. Myra says it's helpful for her to talk things out, yet with all this discussion of art, he's starting to think like Vincent Van Gogh—he'd like to lop off at least one ear.

Evidence points to sexual differences in style of approaching personal problems. Women often talk about their troubles to feel connected and to come to an understanding of the issue with a friend's sympathetic listening. Men often prefer to bring up a problem only when they're interested in tackling and solving it. Men feel baffled that women find some payoff in problem indulgence, while women can't fathom why a guy who claims to care gets so impatient about the things that bother her most.

Next time you think you'll scream because you've already given her the perfect solution, reach for the **ASPIRIN** instead, and cure your headache.

Medicine for being weary of woes

Accept that sharing problems is her tool for building a close relationship, and that she really benefits from just talking. Listening truly offers her more comfort than ingenious solutions.

Structure the problem dialogue by saying how much you do or don't want to discuss.

"Could we not talk about work over dinner?"

"How about if we just relax now and delve into your fresco fantasies over the weekend?"

Probe. You can help her insights along by asking interested questions.

"Well, what kind of work environment *is* more your style?"

"How are frescoes more interesting than painting on canvas?"

Identify your true reaction and state it tactfully—before she realizes the wall might be more responsive.

"I'm finding it hard to listen when you go on and on about your hidden artistic potential. I think it's time to start taking courses already."

Refer her to another person to talk about the issue. Other listeners may have more stamina than you.

"Monica is a good person to talk to about job interviews."

Interest her in a solution if you can do it without pontificating.

"Do you want to hear my ideas about moving ahead in your department?"

"How about using the basement as your studio?"

Name your differences in the way you approach problems. This way you'll understand why it's hard for each of you to do what the other wants.

"You and your friends talk about everything bothering you. Personally, I don't feel comfortable being so open about what's wrong."

"We're different. I'd just go sign up for the course even if I wasn't sure it was the best one. It seems you spend a lot more time making decisions."

I can't express anger with my partner.

Since partnership inevitably involves some conflict, it's essential to be able to say your piece in a peace-promoting way. Jovanny and Greta, two photographers on the quiet side, spent much of their free time around the house, Jovanny reading and Greta in her darkroom. Jovanny brought up the issue of getting out of the house, or at least out of the darkroom, several times, but Greta didn't respond to his suggestions of weekend walks or rides. Though anger was somewhat an alien feeling for Jovanny, after a month of turned-down requests to get out of the house, he realized he felt peeved that Greta remained "in the dark" about his needs. Yet he worried that expressing anger would damage the comfort they felt with each other.

Before learning how to express anger constructively, Jovanny needed to understand some basics about this potent emotion.

1. Feeling angry from time to time is normal in all close human relationships.
2. An expression of anger in itself will not hurt a couple. But the angry expression of anger can.
3. You have the ability to choose when and how you deal with anger.
4. Your partner will not necessarily understand your position and change her behavior, but she's less likely to change if you say nothing constructive at all.
5. Expressing anger is productive when there's a possibility of solving the problem and you have the self-possession to plan how you'll raise your issues. When you meet these conditions, you're ready to plot a scenario.

35

How to live happily angry ever after

1. *Set the scene*. Tell your partner you want to talk and give a brief reason why. Be sensitive to time and place. You're better off bringing up a gripe when both you and your significant other are relaxed and in a calm mood. This way, you're more likely to get agreement to listen.

"Greta, I want to talk to you about something that's important to me."

"Ross, when you have a minute I want to talk about something that will help our money situation."

"Karen, there's something bugging me that I want us to talk about."

2. *Introduce your topic with "I's."* Instead of speaking about what your partner is doing wrong, use statements that begin with the word "I" plus a verb.

I'm   upset
        concerned
        worried
     *hurt
        feeling left out
        sad
    *disappointed
     angry
     frustrated
     irritated
     annoyed
     furious

Note: Since hurt often underlies anger, you might be more truthful and get a better response using the starred words.

Instead of "What kind of life is this—our existence together is the pits!" Jovanny said, "I'm disappointed that we haven't spent time together outside the house. Let's do something about it."

3. *Present your story*. Describe how the situation is affecting you, your life together, the kids, the family. Be descriptive versus accusatory.

"When we don't get out of the house, I start to feel very restless. Also, I think it's important for us to add some variety to our weekends."

4. *Give your partner a turn*. Quit talking and listen to what your partner has to say. If you've avoided hostility, a reasonable partner may just come up with a solution. Don't be surprised, though, if your partner becomes hostile, angry, or defensive. After all, you've just suggested that her loved one thinks something is wrong. But if you remain calm, you'll have a better chance of going on to the next step. (See "I wish I could defuse my partner's explosions of anger." [p. 39] for ways to help her cool down.)

Greta claimed with some irritation that the weekend was the only time she could do enlargements. Jovanny acknowledged her concern and repeated his.

"I know that the weekend is an important time for you to do enlargements. It's also the best time for us to get out of the house together a little bit."

5. *Suggest a resolution*. Bring up a change in actions or attitudes you'd like from your partner. Keep in mind that attitudes won't shift as a result of one discussion.

"I'd like it if we made some plans to go to an inn in the wine country one weekend in November. What do you think?"

6. *Close the discussion.* If it's so far so good—you've at least been heard, and at most come up with a couple of solutions—offer appreciation to your partner.

"I'm glad we got to talk this out, Greta."

"I'm not as angry now. Thanks."

I wish I could defuse my partner's explosions of anger.

If your partner's anger targets something specific that you did, ("How could you forget to confirm our plans with the Dunns?") your challenge is less to defuse than to discuss the issue. (See "I don't take criticism from my partner well." [p. 75] on how to respond to a scolding without escalating into armed conflict.)

But explosions, versus expressions, of anger can damage and even threaten a relationship. When reason flies out the window, your only recourse is to try and weather the emotional storm. (If you worry about literally living through your partner's anger, you need help beyond communication strategies. That's abuse.) When emotions, not reason, rule, deescalating, defusing, and not making a bad situation worse become top priorities.

Charlie and Joan were finally beginning a project they had talked about for many years, a newsletter for parents in their area. With the favorable community reaction, Joan felt pressure to publish a higher quality product with each issue. Exhausted from her perfectionistic standards, Joan began to rage at Charlie before each deadline for getting her involved with something over her head in the first place. Charlie wanted to know the best way to act when his wife lost control. I told him not to get even but to get **M-A-D.**

M-A-D strategies for defusing anger

Moderate your response to the anger. No matter how aggravated you feel, don't—
  • yell back, call him names, bring up everything that

was ever wrong. Trouble always multiplies when one mad person turns into two.
- tell her to calm down if you've noticed this makes things worse.
- interpret fury as an indication that your relationship is falling apart. Unfortunately, some people only allow anger to erupt with people they trust.

The age-old tactic of counting to ten does help many people maintain control. When you're on the verge of raging back, you can also try talking to yourself with thoughts like:

"She's under a lot of pressure this month."

"Here we go. He always goes nuts when he can't find his checkbook."

"One of us has to act mature."

"I'm about to blow up, but if I don't yell or slam doors she calms down sooner."

Acknowledge and **A**ssert. Acknowledge the anger reaction as making sense to your partner, then assert that it is not helping the situation. Here are two examples:

(Acknowledge) "I can see that you're upset that Fred borrowed the car."

(Now assert) "But I don't think screaming at me will get it back in time."

(Acknowledge) "I know you're angry because I told you I really didn't want to go to Aunt Martha's."

(Now assert) "But it only makes things more tense when you accuse me of being selfish."

Delay. If the anger revolves around an issue that needs discussion, wait for a calmer time to respond. Instead of trying to reason with a raging bully, say things like—

"I'll be happy to discuss this when you're calmer."

"I'm too upset by your yelling to answer your questions."

"Doing taxes is important to me too. But we have to be in a better mood to tackle them."

Your self-respect and your relationship will be safer when only one of you goes off the deep end at once. So if she's going crazy, it's your cue to cool it.

"I'm sorry" isn't in my partner's vocabulary.

Tom and Sara were in an apology deadlock again. Tom wouldn't say he was sorry for doubting Sara's ability to pass the bar exam. Tom insisted that since he had only answered her question of how she would do on the test, he had nothing to apologize for. Sara felt because Tom had hurt her feelings, she deserved an apology and resented him still more for making a fuss over offering one. The more Sara pushed Tom for remorse, the more Tom refused to give in.

To communicators concerned with status (like many males), admission equals submission. Though saying "I'm sorry" may seem like a simple way to patch things up, to the chronically unapologetic saving pride matters more than healing a wounded partner. The price of peace—admitting they were at fault—seems too high to pay. (Some men wince at women's tendency to take apologizing so lightly. To Tom, Sara's willingness to say "I'm sorry" when she sneezed, when she forgot to change the sheets, or when she couldn't serve a five-course dinner to unexpected guests, undercut her strength.) Sara will always have a rough time getting an apology out of Tom, but perhaps, with the right approach, she'll be more likely to hear those two magic words.

Coexisting with a partisan of the Love Story motto

1. *Figure out your own belief*. If you have a partner who holds to the saying, "Love means never having to say you're sorry," you face a rough communication challenge. Reflect on whether or not you have a rule that's just as extreme and rigid. If you believe love means you *always*

have to say you're sorry for the least slight, you haven't the faintest chance of converting someone like Tom to your view.

2. *Prompt, don't push.* Demanding an apology polarizes her and weakens your ability to become understood. Besides, an apology offered at gunpoint usually isn't satisfying—"She doesn't really mean it." Make your request for contrition gentle.

DON'T SAY: "I want an apology now."
TRY: "My feelings are hurt and I'd feel better if you apologized."

DON'T SAY: "You'd better say you're sorry."
TRY: "Let's make up, OK?"

3. *Look for other "sorry signs."* If the two magic words don't tumble easily out of your partner's mouth, look for other indications of regret. Watch for a touch, hug, or show of affection, the timely appearance of your favorite treat, or the nonapologizing partner bringing up the sore subject in a reconciliatory way. A few days after their fight, Tom told Sara she'd probably ace the contracts section of the exam, a sure signal that he was sorry.

She can't stand it when
I give her advice.

In Nan and Billy's house it goes like this:

Nan: I wish I could find a cause to get into, maybe volunteering or just doing something worthwhile.

Billy: So call the College Club—I heard they need help, and the hospital gift shop might be looking for volunteers.

Nan: Forget it, you don't even know what I'm interested in.

Billy: Geez! Why bring it up if you don't want my opinion?

Billy means well, and his ideas might be valid, but Nan finds his approach annoying. In giving advice you anoint yourself as an authority, and if no one asked for it, you come across as a know-it-all. More important, like many women, Nan is seeking emotional strokes, not solutions, from her partner. She wants Billy simply to understand and appreciate her problem. This doesn't figure to Billy or to many men who consider belaboring woes a waste of time. He wants her to take action, while she wants a comforting reaction.

If you play Billy's part repeatedly in your household, with Nan's retort, you need to drop the role of adviser. Here are some ideas for not compounding your partner's anguish.

From solution man to solace man

1. *Trust that when she wants your advice, she'll ask for it.* Chances are, she feels capable of saying "I want to hear your opinion" or "Can I get some advice on this?"

2. *When you feel advice coming to your lips,* substitute a response she'll find more helpful, such as:

- Restating what she said or feels in a different way: "Sounds like you're not feeling overloaded any more."
- Relating a similar incident: "That's how I felt when we first moved here."
- Really listening: Just hear her out, nod, and show interest.
- Raising a question: Get her moving in the direction of a solution, but let *her* provide the answer, not you.
  "What kind of volunteering interests you?"
  "So what are some of the options?"
- Reassuring: "That's great. I'm sure there are lots of places that could use your talents."

Warning: If you've been playing solution man for ages, withdrawal symptoms—anxiety, fidgeting, tongue cramps —may accompany your attempt to learn new lines. Take a deep breath. Advice addiction is only in your mind.

She asks for constant reassurance that I care. It's draining.

A partner who doesn't understand or appreciate your way of showing you care may express insecurity by asking for explicit confirmation. By hearing that you still love her, she's reassured that things remain as they were. In her mind, asking you to indulge her with a fuzzy coo or two is an unremarkable request. But many partners experience demands for cuddly words as draining, irritating, and even incomprehensible. Men in particular may find demands for verbal expressions of affection and a partner's neediness difficult to take.

Oliver described his frustration with Kim like this: "Out of the blue, when nothing's wrong, she'll ask, 'Do you still love me?' I resent the pressure to prove myself and usually say something that gets her upset, like, 'Yeah, sure, OK.' Then I resent how insecure she is and she hates how insensitive I am. And the worst of it is that everything was fine until she challenged the way things were going."

How to help the needy one in your life

1. *Assume she doesn't understand the ways you do show your commitment.* Though it's frustrating to have to spell it out for someone who supposedly knows you well, try.

"When I suggest a weekend together away from the kids or when I pick up your Mom at the airport, I'm showing that I care."

"To me, things like staying in bed together till noon on Sunday show how I feel."

2. *Quit reacting to his requests as if you've been asked to jump off a bridge.* Though your gut reaction is to fend him off, understand that this will escalate his neediness and increase tension in the relationship. Rather than push him away, educate him on the effect of his pressure.

"I get really irritated when you ask me how much I care about you."

"I like to talk about my feelings spontaneously, not when I'm pushed."

"I do care and it drives me crazy that you don't realize it after all this time."

3. *Give more—whatever you can emotionally afford.* Though it's not your responsibility, or even possible, to make your mate secure in the relationship, you can initiate a change or two to meet her needs. Figure out or ask what would make her more confident about your caring. You may be assuming that she wants a total transformation of your personality when a few easy changes would improve the situation.

Kim told Oliver she'd feel more cherished if he initiated saying, "I love you," complimented her occasionally on her achievements at work, or talked more at dinnertime. After he complied with suggestions two and three, he found that Kim focused less on getting number one.

If I say yea, he says nay, and it gets me down.

Paula called her live-in partner "Negative Nick" because of his habit of looking at the down side. Once she came home from work excited about the video telephones her company had installed for better communication with long-distance clients. Nick wasted no time saying that the phones were "just a fad" and predicted that her enthusiasm would fizzle within a week. Feeling flattened, Paula wondered how to make Nick understand that his pessimism was having an effect on her optimism about him.

When a mate is perennially pessimistic, don't take it personally. Your partner is expressing a perspective about the world, not necessarily you. Men like Nick view life through dark-colored glasses, perhaps from being conditioned to mistrust people and situations in the "jungle out there." Paired with someone who wears rose-colored lenses, a partner may turn up the negativity as a way of protecting the innocent from an overdose of naiveté. When you have a nay sayer in the house, it's possible to put your upbeat outlook to good use. Here are some tips for—

Becoming positive about Mr. or Ms. Negative

1. *Don't take his negative nature too seriously*. Usually the negater doesn't intend hostility. Indeed, Nick's mother advised Paula to take his cynicism as a compliment, since Nick only nixed the comments of people he really cared about.

2. *Resist the urge to respond in kind*. Sticking to your guns as he aims potshots may not match your picture of

romance, but you needn't crumple or return the fire. For example, Paula could stand her ground about the value of picture phones without getting nasty toward Nick for the way he saw things.

3. *Switch the atmosphere with humor*. Paula learned to diffuse her desire to argue back (and create tension she disliked) by teasing Nick.

"Thanks for your support, Mr. Negative."

"I'm glad to see we're in agreement again."

"I guess we won't be getting picture phones for Christmas."

4. *Bring out the up side of the downer*. If her negativity threatens your well-being, these strategies may bring out her more agreeable side.

• Shelve the Mary Poppins routine. Nothing brings out the sour comments in this type like sugary enthusiasm. No matter how upbeat you feel, tone down the thrill of it all when you spill news to him.

• Be negative first, turning what you really think upside down. Knowing Nick's usual reaction, Paula could announce, "We installed these new picture phones at work. We'll probably spend twenty thousand on them and then stick them in a closet in three months." Nick, of course, would respond, "What do you mean? Those phones are the cutting edge. In fact, we should consider investing in them." Zap! She would have gotten Mr. Negative.

• Invite his opposition. You may feel more control if you extend an invitation to nitpick. In bringing up the picture phones, Paula could say things like:

"You'll probably think this is a bad idea . . ."

"I know how much you hate new technology . . ."

"Lots of people think we made a bad investment . . ."

He talks a lot in public and is the silent type at home.

Anne felt like strangling Victor. For a year, whenever she'd tried to get him to discuss remodeling the kitchen, his only response was "someday." So she couldn't believe it when Victor took center stage at a neighborhood block party, expounding on do-it-yourself versus contracting, wood versus formica, and his plan to double the cabinet space in their kitchen. On the way home from the party, she snipped, "Are we really going to get a new kitchen or were you only showing off for the neighbors?"

Victor's tendency to become more personable in social situations than at home is shared by some men but few women. According to one researcher, men don't like to tell jokes unless they have an audience of at least two people. Female joke tellers, in contrast, prefer one or at most two listeners. The explanation lies with differences in the way men and women view conversation.

In both private and public situations, women use conversation to create and solidify relationships. At home, with their most significant other, their desire to engage in conversation is high. Men, on the other hand, often approach social and couples communication differently. Some men seize the spotlight at a party because they view telling jokes or stories or imparting expertise as a chance to gain attention and status. At home, however, comfortable with status and assured of attention from their mate, many men lose the desire to maintain conversation. From their point of view, it's a compliment, not an insult, that they feel secure enough not to have to show off. As Victor told Anne, "After wooing real estate investors all day at the office, I enjoy coming home and being able to relax without talking."

Here's how to cope with your party animal:

1. *Remember that your instincts are different*. He talks to get attention. You talk to create and confirm closeness.

2. *Respect your different party hats*. As long as he hasn't humiliated you or put you down, don't criticize. Just as you wouldn't want him to make fun of you for not being the life of the party, don't fault him for his natural tendencies.

3. *Extend an invitation*. Capitalize on his social prowess by inviting him to do more of the same at home. Anne would have been better off saying,
"You sure do know a lot about kitchens. I'd appreciate you going into all the options for me at home."

4. *Get him in the mood*. Press his expressive buttons by simulating a situation that may arise socially. Try these motivators:

   • Competition. "Jim Brown said that wooden kitchens last longer."
   "I notice that all the other houses on our block have updated kitchens."
   • Attention. Stop giving him so much and see what happens.
   • Flattery. If you're living with the life of the party, you may be able to cajole him into performing at home.
   "I missed most of that story about the couple who spent forty thousand on a fifteen thousand dollar kitchen. Jerry said it was one of your best."

Why can't I read people the way she does?

Jeff and Nina were at a Christmas party all of thirty seconds when Nina whispered in Jeff's ear, "I think Joan [one of the women in Jeff's office] is getting divorced." Jeff thought Nina was nuts, but a week later Joan herself told him that she had separated from her husband. When Jeff asked his mystical wife how she knew, Nina said, "Easy. She looked relaxed, had a great new haircut, and was playing with her wedding ring."

For centuries, women's interpersonal discernment has been acknowledged as "women's intuition." Now researchers have confirmed females' superior skill in interpreting gestures, posture, and facial expressions from fifth grade through adulthood. Since men in traditionally female professions like teaching and nursing excel in mood reading too, it's not due to chromosomes but to socialization in pleasing others and practice in adjusting to others' moods.

When one partner proves less adept at deciphering communication clues, the more intuitive one may falsely assume that the other just doesn't care. The less intuitive partner tends to complain, "How the heck can I know what she's feeling? Am I supposed to be a mind reader?" By tuning in to each other's strengths and weaknesses, intuitively mismatched partners can close the mood-reading gap.

Tips for the intuitively impaired

1. *Intuition is not associated with intelligence.* So there's nothing wrong with your brain, pal. Explain to your partner that reading moods isn't among your talents.

2. *Intuition does improve with practice*. Start to pay attention to facial expressions, postures, and gestures in the people around you.

- Look at people from a distance and form an impression of what mood they might be in.
- Turn down the sound on the TV. Guess what feeling the actors are conveying, then turn it up and see if you're right.
- Take a stab at guessing how your partner might feel. Even if you're way off, he'll appreciate the effort.

"You look a little down today."

"I bet things went well at your meeting today."

"Something bugging you?"

Note: Expressive people are easier to read, so don't practice with stone-faced types at first.

And to the intuitively gifted

1. *Don't read into every move and expression your partner makes*. This over-vigilance will make you a first class pain.

2. *Don't assume others can read you as well as you read them*. Many people, especially men, need a clear message about your feeling state.

3. *Avoid testing your mate to see if he notices your mood*. It would be nice if he picked up on every nonverbal nuance, but don't act neglected if that doesn't happen.

53

4. *Use your gift wisely, to understand, not to reprimand.*

DON'T SAY: "You're bored again. Can't you get a hobby?"

TRY: "Stumped about what to do again today?"

How do I get across my need to be alone?

Healthy relationships include both time together and time apart. Although some couples go into a relationship with similar togetherness needs, for many others the together/apart quotient becomes a source of conflict. After living together for six months, Harry and Hayley came close to calling it quits because of a tug of war over closeness. Hayley looked forward to spending evenings with Harry just relaxing in front of the VCR. If Harry was involved with a woodworking project in the basement, she liked to go downstairs and watch him. Harry couldn't understand the allure of simply sitting together on the same couch. As for Hayley's penchant for watching him, he felt she would be better off with hobbies of her own. Feeling claustrophobic from Hayley's coziness cravings, Harry made the painful decision to move to his own place.

After three lonely weeks, Harry realized that he and Hayley belonged together—just not every waking hour. He knew things would be better between them if Hayley recognized his need for some S - P - A - C - E.

Getting together about being apart

Sort it out. Figure out your need for solitary time and how it seems to differ from your partner's.

> I need one night out a week with my friends and Sunday afternoon reading quietly. Richard seems to like spending every night and weekend together.

Present your preferences to your mate. She'll listen to the extent that you don't attack or grumble. Pick a time to talk when tension is low. Say what you've noticed, then state your need.

"Whenever I go bowling on Wednesdays it seems like you get annoyed. It's important for me to bowl at least once a week for relaxation."

Ask for what you want from your partner.

"I'd like to be able to do my woodworking without feeling pressure to talk."

"I need your support so I don't feel guilty the whole time I'm bowling."

Compromise. Since she has needs too, negotiation is the next step. Don't be surprised if bringing up this topic brings out strong feelings. Mates who feel their closeness quota has not been met may resent you, no matter how tactful you've been.

Step One: Let her let off steam.

Harry: "What do you think? Can we get this thing straight?"

Hayley: "I'm tired of being in last place after your woodworking and twelve other hobbies. I want someone who's there for me."

Step Two: Encourage her to say what she would like and what degree of togetherness she would accept. *Listen*. Till now you've focused only on your side.

Harry: "So what do you suggest that might work for both of us?"

Hayley: "I'd at least like us to watch a movie or spend some time relaxing together before we go to bed."

Ease into a new understanding. Although neither of you can change your attitudes or basic needs, you can adapt for the sake of the relationship. Agree to handle your need to be apart in a more together way.

Harry: "OK, I'll try to finish up with my hobbies by ten so we can watch a movie or something. Meanwhile, can you do something on your own while I'm busy?"

After their negotiation, Hayley weaned herself from watching Harry's woodworking and started to read more. Harry was able to concentrate on his projects and felt better about relaxing with Hayley. With less tension about togetherness, they were ready to talk about The Big M —making their arrangement permanent.

I like to talk things over after a fight, and she doesn't.

Though their fights were infrequent (and usually over how expenses should be split), Lily thought her live-in partner Peter had a peculiar way of patching things up. After pacing around the house and slamming a few doors, Peter would act as if nothing had happened. Peter's argumentative amnesia aggravated Lily. She wanted to debrief and figure out some way to prevent the next money argument. Peter resisted her suggestions, saying he preferred not to "rehash everything again."

If all relationships include conflict, many include conflict over the aftermath of spats. Women, often more comfortable with compromise and negotiation and uneasy with lingering tension, may have greater motivation to clear the air. Accustomed to combative conversation, men may be more likely to go full force into a fight and then feel fine after they cool down. To avoid post-skirmish skirmishes, partners should consider—

The peace treaty (Making peace with how your partner makes peace)

Given that each faction has unique customs and communications regarding the formation of said peace treaty, the following resolutions should be invoked post-battle:

Resolution One. Hold down the fort. Watch the enemy's moves for several hours after the clash. Keep an eye out for signs which indicate the battle is over (she resumes normal activities, stops sulking or storming, or hoists a white flag).

Resolution Two. Invite the foe to break bread and discuss the incident—after you recover from battle injuries. A 24-to-48-hour waiting period is usually necessary. Expect resistance to the proposal, and persist. Don't start a new battle by blaming rather than sharing the fault.

Resolution Three. Focus on working it out, not winning. Describe in calm terms what you learned from the incident and how you two warring parties see things differently. Invite her to share her perspective.

"I find it exhausting to argue about expenses each month."

"You don't want a fifty-fifty split, but I think it's the only fair way. How do you see it?"

Warning: If you see a glaze in her eyes, that's a spoiler for talking things over. Do not shoot. You may need another waiting period.

Resolution Four. When your goal is some change in the relationship, lay the options on the line. Try to get his agreement on one point or at least acknowledgment of the possibilities.

"I don't want to fight over this any more. I see three things we can do differently: try splitting expenses fifty-fifty for three months, split some expenses fifty-fifty and not others, or I pay the rent and you pay everything else. So what do you think?"

Resolution Five. Don't escalate to World War III if she doesn't want to talk it over. Partners may end up in a stalemate where no amount of discussion will change entrenched positions. If the first four resolutions fail, you're walking in a minefield on this issue. Either prepare for another no-win contest or get ready to surrender.

Need more motivation to make peace? In a study of twenty-five marriages lasting twenty-five years or more, a Florida researcher found that the ability to solve problems together was the best predictor of marital success.

I have to walk on eggshells when I talk to her.

Lynda, a stock trader and mother of five-year-old twins and a teenager, said that with all the stress in her life, she felt headed for a meltdown. No wonder Mike, her more mellow husband, felt he would be nuked for any conversation more demanding than "Hi, hon, how was your day?" Actually, Lynda did once snarl back, "Now I have to give a blow-by-blow account of my day? I wish everyone would leave me alone."

There are several reasons why your partner may be prone to react off the Richter scale, misinterpreting just about everything you say. Sometimes, as with Lynda, her world is a pressure cooker, and even the most pleasant addition to the pot makes her boil over. Secondly, your partner's anger or resentment toward you for unresolved grievances (you don't respect his privacy enough) may emerge in hairtrigger responses, rather than explicit complaints. It's also possible that your style is unintentionally provocative. For example, when Mike tells Lynda the kids left their toys all over the kitchen and then starts to get into bed, she shouts, "So why didn't you just get off your butt and clean things up?" Men like Mike, unable to protest when an innocent comment gets misconstrued or turned against them, find themselves clamming up. Some even confess to talking in half-truths, since any statement that could remotely be seen as a reproach could set off an explosion.

If you've been tiptoeing around an overreactor, do continue to tread lightly while you try out some new steps.

Eggsercises for eggshell walkers

1. *Don't eggsaggerate the power of his/her reaction.* Some partners act grouchy to let off steam in a safe place, and then bounce back if you ignore a callous comment or two. Lynda would get fired for chewing out her clients, but Mike was likely to stick around despite her outbursts.

2. *Eggsplain, eggsplain, eggsplain.* Overreactors may quickly take your comments out of context or read in what you never meant. Explosion prevention requires you to explain what you don't mean as well as what you do.

"I'm not saying that you or I should go clean up right now, but the twins keep leaving their toys all over the kitchen."

Other eggsplanatory phrases:

"Don't think I'm blaming you . . ."
"Don't take this personally, but . . ."
"Don't take this the wrong way, but . . ."
"I'm not sure how to say this, but . . ."

3. *Eggsamine your communication strategies.* You may be using inflammatory language, tone, or facial expressions while claiming to be oh so innocent. Examine yourself for—

- condescending tone, whining
- frowning or hostile face
- either overdirect or indirect statements (See "He's too blunt/She never gets to the point." [p. 153])
- authoritarian or accusatory language ("You ought, you should, you never, you better")
- bringing up sore subjects at bad times (Mike tended to go into his "house is messy" discourse just as Lynda was sitting down with an after-dinner glass of wine)

- complaining as if your partner was supposed to make things better ("If you put some effort into it, we could have more contact with our relatives.")

4. *Eggspress yourself anyway*. Although no one is the perfect diplomat in intimate conversations, if you've followed the above guidelines, you're probably on more solid footing. Then as you get off the eggshells, she'll crack less.

Mike learned to give Lynda at least twenty minutes of space when she first got home and to make fewer comments about what they should do around the house. In turn, Lynda offered more loving reactions and they lived happily ever after, surrounded by the twins, their teenager, and a lot of old eggshells.

How do I react to my partner's jealousy?

Partners express jealous thoughts in response to a real or imagined threat to the relationship. If you openly flirt or pursue others, your partner is responding to reality and you face the choice of changing your behavior or changing your mate. If you're sure that jealous eruptions spring from distorted impressions (You'd be friendly to the Tom Selleck-like letter carrier even if he looked like Elmer Fudd) or unfounded fantasies (Her ex cheated on her and on your photography club night out, she can't help thinking you are too), you can minimize the likelihood of a jealous reaction. Since jealousy can be both complex and destructive—one survey showed that for more than a third of couples in marital therapy, jealousy was an issue—you may also need to accept the fact that the green monster will rear its ugly head no matter what you do.

At their monthly square dance, Al had a fit when he noticed Gayle do-si-doing very close to Fred. According to Al, Gayle was making "unnecessary body contact" with Fred, the new guy in their square. Finding Al's charges ridiculous, Gayle claimed that she couldn't be accountable for every body part during a do-si-do or a promenade. She announced that she'd rather quit square dancing than put up with Al's paranoia. Perhaps she should try some jealousy prevention tactics first.

Defanging the green monster

1. *Extend an open invitation.* Make him feel wanted by inviting his inclusion in your activities whenever possible. Gayle learned to ask Al along on bowling night, even though the game wasn't up his alley. Al stayed home

but fretted less, reasoning, "If she asked me along she couldn't possibly be flirting her way through the tenth frame."

2. *Sign in, please.* Make efforts to check in when you're not around. Even better, bring back physical evidence of your whereabouts when you're without him. Hold on to those score sheets or class handouts.

3. *Predict the sore spots.* If you're in a social situation, anticipate any jealousy jostlers—the boss who makes very intense eye contact, the presence of your ninth-grade girlfriend at the high school reunion. Then prepare him or her.

"My boss Baird is a real character. He always stares at people in this weird intense way."

"Oh, there's Brenda from ninth grade. I can hardly recognize her. You look about fifteen years younger than she does."

4. *Pick up the pieces, if you know he's seen red.* You couldn't help it that the palm reader said you were having an affair with a six-foot bald man, and your short, hairy partner overheard and stormed out of the party. These tough situations call for tough tactics.

• Acknowledge that he's upset, but don't get upset yourself.

DON'T SAY: "What's wrong with you? You can't possibly believe a palm reading—it's just for fun."

TRY: "I can see that what Madame Futura said upset you. I wish she'd never opened her mouth."

• Reassure her simply and calmly—with the truth.

"Come on, you know you're my one and only."

"I wasn't even aware of touching Fred during the do-si-do."

• Apologize—not for your innocent actions but for being misperceived.

"I'm sorry if laughing on the phone with my boss upset you."

"I'm sorry if you thought I was dancing too close to Fred."

How do I express my need for affection?

We're not all blessed with a sensuous special someone, and it's common for couples to desire different amounts of cooing and cuddling. When he offers only an iota of your affectional quota, frustration and feelings of rejection can set in. Take heart in knowing that his reticence in showing affection doesn't signal low attraction. Nor does the couple falling all over each other near you in the movies necessarily have a stronger bond.

Charlie came from a family of kissers. His girlfriend, Elaine, thought she'd scream when his Great Aunt Belle gave her a smooch at a family affair. When she told Charlie that Aunt Belle was all wet, he blasted Elaine for being an ice woman who hadn't given him a kiss on her own initiative in their five years together. Wrong approach, Charlie!

You're walking a tightrope here. Expressing your needs makes sense, but be careful not to diminish affectional feelings when you're trying to inspire more demonstrativeness.

Getting the cool one to cuddle

1. *Cool it yourself.* If you're always initiating, she has little space to let her own urges for affection well up. Worse, she may feel smothered. (See "My partner likes to touch me all the time." [p. 70])

After their blowout, Charlie cooled it for almost a week—due to anger, not self-control. But when Elaine ran all the way into the garage to get a good-bye kiss, Charlie realized he'd never let her needs build up till she felt ready to express them.

2. *Try flattery*. Try letting him know how good something does or would feel. Emphasize his ability to please rather than your desire to be pleased.

"You have the most comforting hand to hold."

"Remember that time in 1968 when you gave me a massage?"

"When we cuddle in bed in the morning, that makes my whole day."

The next two techniques won't bring out her natural affectional instincts (if they exist), so use them only if you'll be satisfied with artificially induced affection. As Charlie remarked, "Heck, even a bribed hug is better than no hug at all."

3. *Negotiate nuzzling*. Here you suggest exchanges you can make. With awareness of your differing needs, you invite flexibility for mutual satisfaction.

"Harry, I'd like my back rubbed. I know you don't like to have yours rubbed, but what can I do in exchange for a ten-minute massage?" This is how Harry finally got the basement cleaned.

4. *Lay it all out*. The most direct approach may be appropriate for those truly feeling frustrated. You state what you like, what you don't like and see what happens. Use this approach only when you're not mad. As we saw with Charlie, demanding affection in an angry way is a surefire way of maintaining distance.

"Elaine, I'm tired of always being the affectionate one in our relationship. I'd enjoy more signs of closeness from you, like a kiss good-night, or holding hands when we walk down the street."

If after trying the above, you're convinced you'll be affectionally neglected for life in this relationship, you have three options:

- Change your expectations.
- Get your needs met elsewhere (treat yourself to a therapeutic massage twice a month).
- Cope with the frustration by coddling yourself more.

During his week of abstinence, Charlie built the aquarium he'd always talked about, and spent less time thinking about the cold fish he lived with.

My partner likes to touch me all the time.

Individual affectional needs form from many factors, including early role models, culture, and the newness of a relationship. Because the intensity of initial infatuation may mask a partner's true affectional needs, the common complaint arises: "He used to be so romantic." Keep in mind as well that someone's mushy-gushy needs show up in relation to a particular partner. Since Gordon hated the way his first wife constantly shouldered him away, he was surprised when his second wife's almost hourly demands for a "major hug" overwhelmed him.

Though it may seem masochistic to be the adorer all the time, some of us do enjoy reaching rather than being reached for. In turn, the aloof mate maintains the more powerful position of being the beloved rather than the lover. Trouble arises, however, when the reacher causes the more restrained partner to feel suffocated. New mom Jan found attending to her baby's demands taxing and tiring. Though she appreciated husband James for doing his share, she couldn't stand his constant stroking and surprise hugs each evening. She didn't want him to feel rejected but wished fervently for a stretch of time when no other human being was touching her.

Expressing yourself on a touchy subject

1. *Fragile—handle with care*. Your mate may judge your closeness as a couple by the number of hugs and kisses per day. Assuring him that even though you feel close, you just don't always need to *be* close should help.

2. *Send the right message*. If you feel like flinching, don't smile when she's pinching. Efforts to be polite may be misperceived as approval. Send-off messages to use:

- Flinch. Make an abrupt movement when she makes her move.
- Startle. Put on a surprised expression.
- Shield. Put an object between you and her. Men have used a newspaper for this purpose for centuries.
- Stop sign. "Say "not now," or "I'm concentrating," or "hold it.""

A secure and sensitive partner may respond to these signals for space, but . . .

3. *Special delivery may be required*. Consider more urgent methods if your tactile differences interfere with day-to-day comfortability and if he seems oblivious to the signals suggested above.
- Stamp of approval. Be explicit about what is or what isn't comfortable for you, when, where, and how.
"I get nervous if someone is all over me when I'm driving."
"I need help with the housework, not more touching after a long day with the baby."
"I'm embarrassed when you ask me for a kiss in front of the guys."
- C.O.D. (Control of Delivery). Come up with a compromise that satisfies both her ache for affection and your need to cool it.
"We can cuddle before bedtime but I can't be interrupted when I'm at the computer."
"How about one big hug and then I'd like to read the paper while you feed the baby."
"One smooch in the morning and one when I come home is plenty for me, OK?"

How do I give criticism without starting a battle?

If you're trying to help and your critiques lead to warfare, something is wrong. Your mate may be a critically sensitive type. (See "I don't take criticism from my partner well." [p. 75]) Perhaps your delivery gets his defenses up. Rather than hearing a plug for his betterment, he finds the barrage biting. Or maybe you're just too picky and your less-than-perfect partner is protecting his freedom to be himself without your assistance.

Faultfinding is not confined to either sex and it's common for one partner in a relationship to be more correcting than accepting. Though researchers have learned that women are more critical of the quality of their relationship as a whole than their mates, men's tendency to be blunt and to view criticism as "nothing personal" can distress their partners. Likewise, a man's need to feel accepted and independent in self-improvement makes suggestions seem to him like mudslinging. In his illuminating book, *What Men Won't Tell You but Women Need to Know*, author Bob Berkowitz begins a chapter on "How to criticize a man" with one word of advice—"Don't."

Maryellen and Sal had a never-ending battle over driving. When Maryellen drove, Sal complained she was too cautious, with one foot always on the brake. Sal, on the other hand, drove like a speed demon, with Maryellen expressing fears for her life. Each resented the other telling them what to do. Naturally they and their kids did not enjoy many peaceful drives together. For less bumpy going, they needed some tutoring in how to disagree without driving each other and the kids nuts.

A short course in criticism

1. *Before you get started, assess the situation.* First decide if it's worth bringing up what's bugging you. Don't turn the key in the ignition unless you can answer "yes" to one or more of the following questions.

- Will the criticism help my partner?
- Is the criticism about something he or she can change?
- Are there more benefits from speaking up than for not speaking up?
- Is this a good time and place to talk?

2. *Map your route.* When you're dealing with a sensitive subject and a sensitive mate, you need to plan your approach or you'll get trapped in a thunderstorm. Include these elements in your critical approach:

- genuine concern for his or her well-being
- a positive tone and wording
- clear expression of your destination—what you want to happen

3. *Leave deadly weapons behind.* Don't expect to reach your goal with any of the following:

- blaming or put-downs

"You'll be arrested if you don't drive as fast as the other cars."

"See these gray hairs? It's because of your reckless driving."

- harsh or angry tone (you can *be* angry but try not to sound that way)
- ultimatums and threats

"If you don't slow down, I'll never take a trip with you again."

"Go ahead and speed. I'll get carsick all over your suede seats."

4. *Stick to safe territory*. If you decide to go ahead and criticize, play it safe or run the risk of ruining the ride. Here are some sound methods:

• Accept and redirect. Show acceptance of the way she currently does her thing and then suggest a way that's even better.

"I know you like to drive carefully, and that's great. I think you'll be safer if you look ahead and use the brake less."

"I love the fact that you're ambitious. If you're going to volunteer for extra work, maybe you could plan your workload so you'll still be able to go to Billy's Little League games on Saturdays."

• Make it your problem. Let him show you the way to solve it. That's right. Although he's the one snoring, you're the one tossing and turning because of it. Carefully describe your plight, using the pronoun "I" whenever possible.

"I'm a light sleeper, so is there some way I can let you know when you're snoring?"

"I have this thing about well-done meat. I keep forgetting to let you know that when we're barbecuing."

"I have a really sensitive stomach, so I wonder if you could slow down a bit."

> If it's not working but no one can fix it
> Don't make it worse by trying to nix it.

74

I don't take criticism from my partner well.

We'd like to think we can do no wrong in our loved one's mind, but expecting unconditional condoning is unrealistic once we're past the fawning stage. Your partner isn't perfect, right? Neither are you. A barrage of unsolicited criticism is never helpful, and if that's what you're getting, you have every right to protest. But occasional constructive criticisms—comments which are clearly motivated by concern for your well-being— deserve a listen if not a welcome mat.

Trusting that you can be less than perfect but still loved is quite a revelation for the critically sensitive. During his first marriage, Steve was peeved that his wife was so accepting and complacent. She never even mentioned his two-pack-a-day cigarette habit. In contrast, Maria, Steve's second wife, nudged him often about self-improvement, with suggestions for everything from karate classes to subliminal messages to help him overcome his bad habits. Steve appreciated Maria's concern for his health but found himself bristling each time she tactfully tried to assist. These suggestions helped him let Maria be helpful.

Are you critically sensitive? (A checklist)

_____ You focus less on the issue and more on the fact that your spouse is "putting you down." Steve realized his defensiveness with Maria deflected attention from his true problems, such as nicotine addiction.

_____ You'd never take his suggestion because it would be giving in. Even if the suggestion was delivered less than delicately, your mate is on your side, not giving you cyanide.

_____ Your mate complains it's difficult or impossible to give you any input. Maria and Steve's initially rational discussion about tobacco ended with her saying, "So go ahead and kill yourself" and Steve retorting, "OK, I will."

If any of the above apply, it's time to harden up a little.

How to act when he'd like a change in your act (Taking it like a grown-up)

1. *Shhh.* Let him spit it out, while you digest. One key question to ask: Does he have my best intentions at heart? If the answer is yes, keep listening.

2. *Control your impulse to throw a tantrum.* Think like a diplomat, not a kid in diapers. Agree with whatever you can agree with, or at least show appreciation for her concern.

"You're right. I should try to quit as a New Year's resolution."

"I know that my smoking is really getting to you and I'm sorry."

3. *Be brave.* If you've mastered step two and feel ready to consider the value of his suggestions, start soliciting his ideas and responding, either positively or negatively.

• Soliciting: "Well, what makes you think this is a good time to stop?"

"What have you heard about group hypnosis for smoking?"

76

- Responding: "Maybe one of us can call and get a brochure about the hypnosis classes."

"With all the changes at work, this would be the worst possible time to quit. I don't think I'm making an excuse, either."

4. *Make nice*. Thank her for being concerned and let her know whether or not you're open to discussion. If not, still be nice when you tell her. After all, she was just trying to help.

"Your ideas sound pretty good. When we get the catalogues we can talk about which method would be best."

"Maria, please do me a favor and don't bring up my habit on a weekly basis. I know I've got the problem and it's up to me to handle it."

If criticism was given in a critical way, you're right to react to his style, not the suggestion. Simply state what put you off.

"I don't appreciate being reprimanded about eating a box of doughnuts as if I'm a two-year-old."

"I'll listen to your suggestions when you can offer them without sounding so angry."

I'd like to help my partner change a bad habit.

Since people change only when they're ready, you're best off letting your mate determine when and how you should coach the change along. Valuing cooperativeness, many women relish a teamwork approach to licking a bad habit. Men, more sensitive to having weak spots exposed and valuing independence more than interdependence, may not respond as well to a we're-in-this-together theme. Some men react as if it's none of your business, even if you're his wife. It's especially important not to give the impression that you care more about the bad habit than he does. Overconcern may sabotage the entire stop-smoking or be-more-communicative-with-the-kids campaign.

Glen wanted to stop snacking and start losing the seventeen pounds he'd gained since a car accident the previous year. His wife Rita, turned off by the tire around his tummy, said she would help him 150 percent. A lifelong calorie counter, Rita volunteered her nutritional knowledge twenty times a day ("Glen, popcorn with butter is no lo-cal snack" and on and on). Glen snapped that he wanted to diet his way and that her comments implied he was an idiot. As Rita watched Glen dip carrot sticks into ultra-fattening dip, she steamed silently, frustrated to know that she had a lot of goodhearted help to offer. But she didn't have to retreat totally. She could have stayed in the helping role once she learned to distinguish cheerleading that motivates and supports from goading, shaming, and badgering.

How to doom his improvement drive

Do any of these and you'll make sure he keeps his objectionable habit for life.

- Mention the habit every waking minute.
- Compare him to other men or women:
    "Orville Pishnowitz dropped twenty pounds in two weeks."
- Tell him he's ruining your life:
    "I hardly have any space when we sit together in the movies."
    "You have a 30 percent greater chance of making me a widow before I'm sixty with that belly."
- Issue ultimatums and threats:
    "Get skinnier by my cousin Carleen's wedding in March or I'm going without you."
- Analyze his hangups:
    "Your mother must not have fed you well enough when you were a child and you're trying to make up for it now."
- Throw a fit every time he backslides:
    "I can't stand it. You didn't have to eat more than a spoonful of that Boston cream pie."
- Brag about your own self-control:
    "I don't know what's so hard about dieting. I could visit a chocolate factory and not take a lick."
- Criticize his lack of self-control:
    "So that's why they wrote 'undisciplined' on your kindergarten report card."

How to zoom her toward success

Follow these three guidelines and she'll change if she wants to.

79

1. *Ask your partner*. Simply ask what you can do to be helpful. Trust that the answer you receive is the truth.

"What can I do to help you stop smoking?"

A follow-up prompt: "Just let me know if there's anything else I can do to help."

2. *Do what she asks*. Remember that different strategies will work for different people. If she doesn't mention throwing out the emergency packs of cigarettes stashed in her drawers, don't take it upon yourself to dispose of them as a way to help.

3. *Acknowledge positive change and effort*. Compliment real change and effort that you notice.

"You smell great these days. And I was impressed with your willpower when you turned down a cigarette when we were having dinner with the Wilsons."

"One month without a smoke, that's terrific! I'm taking you out to your favorite deli."

Even when his habit hurts you more, remember that it's *his* habit and only he has the cure.

How can I get my partner to do something without nagging?

Nagging, or persistent negative tactics used to get somebody to do something, creates an annoying atmosphere. To the poor soul who feels put upon, the nagger is a nuisance. Women frequently find themselves labeled as this sort of pest since men place a premium on independence and tend to hear a request for helpfulness as an infringement. On the other hand, women often feel more comfortable saying yes to requests, since they feel it enhances closeness with their partner. Whenever pleas to lug the groceries in or the garbage out get no results, it's natural to want to raise your volume or complain. Other maneuvers, though, help you persuade without getting on your partner's nerves.

The Brief Nonnagger's Success Manual

1. *Recognize the symptoms of nagging.* These include:

- Even though you're sure she won't do as you ask, you bug her anyway.
- You never ask for something just once.
- You get annoyed by lots of things your partner does and you always have to say so.
- You get no response, the wrong response, or sabotage. (He finally takes the laundry out of the dryer—when the towels are still wet.)
- You often use phrases like "you should," "you ought to," or "you'd better."
- You are perceived as a nag. No matter how sweet your song, nagging is in the ear of the beholder.

2. *Control yourself, not him.* Limit the number of wishes you target to one a day or five a week. Prioritize and choose your gripe goals with your main needs in mind. Resolve not to mention any of the others for the time being. Evelyn wanted Stan's help with keeping the kitchen clean, updating her résumé, and feeding the dog. Most of all, Evelyn hated the clutter created by Stan's baseball-card collection in their one-bedroom apartment and worried about his unbalanced eating habits. Her persuasive concern for the month, she decided, was confining Gehrig and the gang to Stan's corner of their bedroom. Knowing that Stan had once refused his mother's offer of $200 if he would eat a stalk of broccoli, she chose not to focus on his adding vegetables to his diet.

3. *Convey your concern strategically.* Try one of these three gambits, delivered in a neutral tone of voice.

• The happy hint. A casual, subtle, and friendly approach can succeed when the tension surrounding a concern is minimal.

"It would be great if . . . the socks were attached when you put them in the hamper."

"I'd love it if . . . you picked up Jill at daycare on Tuesdays."

"I'm wondering if . . . we could both make it to the condo association meeting this time around."

"Things would be even better if . . . we finished dinner by seven on my bowling night."

• The sure-it's-a-hassle request. Here, you acknowledge how your request might put your partner out. Feeling understood, he might soften sooner.

"I know you have a lot to do after work. Would you be able to pick up the dry cleaning?"

"I know you don't want to watch it, but I'd like it if you could tape the special on assassinations for me."

"Even though you don't like to give things away,

could you try to donate the sweaters you haven't worn since college to the rummage sale?"

• The **N-A-G** approach. For top priority or chronic concerns, nag in a new way. This three-step method lets you influence, not invade.

Name—State what's bothering you without blame.
> "When cards are all over the apartment . . ."

Appraise—State the effect that the concern is having on you.
> ". . . it's hard to keep things organized and looking neat."

Goal-set—State what you would like to happen, your goal.
> "I'd like the cards to stay in the bedroom on your side of the bureau."

4. *Offer praise for doing something right.* Your mate needs to know that his efforts to be helpful are appreciated, even if they're not top priority favors for you. ("Thanks for developing the pictures of our trip.") Noting everyday accomplishments increases the likelihood that he'll hear you next time instead of getting mad.

> It doesn't help to be a drag.
> So be a pleasure, not a nag.

He'll never admit when he needs help.

Nadine considered her boyfriend Ben an enigma. He'd often offer a shoulder to cry on for her women friends who were having relationship problems and had insights which they found particularly perceptive. Yet when Nadine suggested they see a counselor to iron out some long-standing concerns about their relationship, Ben refused, insisting that he'd figure things out on his own. Apparently Ben could give help, but receiving it didn't interest him.

Knowing that your sweetheart could benefit from input that he won't accept (whether from a psychotherapist or from the salesperson in the tie department) can be exasperating. Research shows that women as a group feel more comfortable asking for information, assistance, and support. Women buy most self-help books, ask more for help in stores, and often complain that the men in their lives would rather stay lost in Oshkosh forever than stop at a gas station for directions. As the Nadine and Ben story illustrates, psychotherapists would be out of business if they relied on men as patients. Psychologist Alvin Baraff estimates that only 15 percent of the typical therapist's caseload consists of men in individual therapy.

Why do men resist an assist if they'd come out ahead in the long run? Many women fail to appreciate that men may feel uncomfortable or vulnerable (even in a brief encounter with a tie salesperson or gas station attendant) when they don't have answers and the other person gets to play the role of expert. For them, the discomfort involved in asking for help may outweigh the discomfort of driving aimlessly around Oshkosh or choosing the wrong tie. The price they pay for feeling competent may appear outlandish to a mate comfortable with help seeking.

Helping when your mate won't seek it

1. *Don't play doctor.* You'll get nowhere diagnosing his direction-asking phobia ("You're so insecure you can't stand not being the expert every second") or providing prescriptions ("You need to see a counselor to straighten out your head about marriage"). Remember what the psychiatrist said about the light bulb: He could change it, but only if the light bulb "really wanted to change."

2. *Don't apply pressure.* Toss away the tourniquet technique.
"If you don't stop at the next gas station, I'm never taking a trip with you again."

3. *Do offer a soothing remedy.* Gently lay out the benefits of getting information, support, or advice. Focus on how good things would be if . . . If she bites, great. If not, drop it.
"Things might smooth out for us if we talk to a professional."
"We could save gas and time by stopping and finding out how to get back to Route 66."

4. *Do play the party seeking first aid.* He might come along eventually if you initially take on the role of the one who wants or needs assistance. Remember that pride motivates him to avoid seeking help, so you can act bravely for the two of you while preserving face.
"I know you hate to stop, but if you park across the street from the station, I'll run over and ask."
"I know counseling is foreign to you, but I'd like it if you came to a session just to help me work a few things out."

How can I hint about the gift I'd like?

To many of us, a gift is a tangible symbol of what our partner thinks of us. So when we rate something expensive and carefully chosen, we conclude we're worth a lot in his eyes. On the other hand, if the card was inappropriate and the present something we would give the doorman, we feel we've learned how little we really matter. But in contrast to gift lovers, others value gift buying or receiving hardly at all. These folks usually explain that any once-a-year tribute pales beside the day-to-day giving in a good relationship. If these opposites pair up, watch out, especially on very special occasions.

Sheila felt as thrilled as a six year old when she saw the big box Matt brought home for her fortieth birthday. She had been hoping for a computer that would help her freelance writing career along. When instead she unwrapped a food processor with sixteen attachments she couldn't help letting loose some hot tears. "What did you get me, a food masher?" Matt was devastated and protested, "But now you'll be able to cook all kinds of gourmet food." Sheila grew livid at this. "You mean you got me something that you'll be able to enjoy?" Though Sheila's disappointment was understandable, she could have headed off Matt's bumbling with tactful wish tactics.

For happily-ever-after wish fulfillment

1. *Don't expect magic.* Observe her giving style. After one or two occasions, you should be able to grasp how seriously she takes gifts and the degree to which she understands what you like. Sheila, for instance, could have noticed at her first birthday with Matt that to him a steam iron meant true love.

2. *Risk breaking the spell*. Though it would be nice if he intuitively knew how important the perfect gift is to you, you can up the odds of getting what you'd like by sharing your dream.

"Honey, when I look back, the gifts that stand out are the ones that I wouldn't have bought for myself, like good jewelry or a sexy negligee."

3. *Sprinkle some fairy dust well before the occasion*. Drop a few hints associating the words "birthday" or "anniversary" with a particular item or two.

"Look at this whirlpool—I'd love something like that this anniversary."

"You know, I never owned a cashmere sweater. It would be great to have one this fall."

If he's really a tough case, be crystal clear.

"Matt, this birthday is special, so forget the appliance this year. How about something more romantic and personal, like flowers?"

4. *Enlist the aid of a wizard*. Get his brother, colleague, or best friend to pass a hint on to him for you. Then get ready to grin yourself silly when you unwrap just what you wanted.

She overreacts.

Sonya, a nursing home administrator, was not a first-class chef. When husband Mark good-naturedly said the burger she'd barbecued was raw, Sonya began crying that she "never made anything right." To Mark, Sonya's babyish reaction was a bigger problem than the undercooked burger. When one partner thinks logically ("If the burger is raw let's get it cooked") rather than emotionally ("Sonya might be hurt if I seem to criticize her cooking") and the other partner reacts emotionally ("Woe is me, I'm a klutz in the kitchen") rather than logically ("Let's get that burger back on the grill"), misunderstandings abound. We seem cold, analytical, and distant when we ignore the emotional impact of what we say and do. On the other hand, we seem disorganized, impractical, and irrational when we erupt with feelings and miss the beef of the matter. Though we may forever think and feel differently from a mate, we can still aim for a better meeting of mind and heart.

For balanced responses to emotions—

1. *Use your noodle.* Look at the situation from the other side. If we replay the Sonya and Mark incident, Sonya believes that wives and husbands should make each other feel good, not inadequate. Since this was the third time in a week that Mark mentioned faults with her cooking, she thought he was implying that she was hopeless when it came to cooking. And to Sonya, cooking prowess was somehow linked with her rating as a wife. Although Mark hadn't intended these connections, he could recognize that given these assumptions, her reaction made sense.

The next time you're met with a reaction you don't get, ask yourself, "Where does this emotional reaction come from?" or "What hot button did I press?" rather than "What's wrong with her?" Be especially careful not to sound critical or demanding when he's exhausted, overwhelmed, or hurried.

2. *Don't offer logic when she's emotional.* When someone is highly perturbed, reasoning with them doesn't usually work. Mark compounded his mistake by describing exactly how medium meat looked, felt, and tasted so Sonya would know for the future. When she threw a bun and told him to make his own damn burger, Mark didn't get it. "I was just trying to be helpful!" Muzzling yourself would be a better move, Mark.

3. *Think before you speak.* Unless you don't mind mustard in your face, don't provoke your partner. Avoid saying any of the following:

"You're off your rocker."
"What got into you?"
"You're acting like a nut."
"Are you crazy?"
"Do you have PMS again?"
"I'd better call the men in the white coats."

4. *Later, provide an explanation.* You have a right, after things have settled down a bit, to state how you see things. For example, Mark could say, "I was just talking about how I like my hamburger. It didn't have anything to do with you or your ability to cook." You score bonus points if you are able to show nonjudgmental appreciation of her perspective, as in, "I know I made you really upset when I mentioned the burger, but . . ."

She embarrasses me in public.

Dennis was attracted to Zelda's teasing and flattering manner when they first met, and then learned to love the rather serious and thoughtful woman she was outside of social situations. When her preening party side emerged at his college reunion, Dennis was chagrined. He figured his old buddies would think he was a fool for putting up with such a flirt.

To the extent that we view our partner's behavior as an extension of our own, it can bring out a blush in us. When Zelda flirts with your old frat friends as if she's available or your boyfriend Ricky dominates a dinner party with stories of his past lives in ancient Egypt, it's difficult to distance yourself to think, "Oh, there goes Zelda again," or "That Ricky is a real character, but I still love him."

In truth, the person you're committed to can sometimes make you cringe. Here are some ideas for getting less flustered when your special someone isn't cutting the mustard.

Getting back in the pink when your face is scarlet

1. *Don't do anything.* Even if your beloved is hula dancing on your boss's dining room table, you're still not responsible for his actions. He's your mate, not your child. Scolding or berating shines the spotlight on your embarrassment, and that's likely to make the crowd uncomfortable as well.

2. *Ignore or leave it.* In most social situations, you have the ability to ambulate to a different part of the room. When the hula dance begins, it's a good time to sample the onion dip. You may first want to note other folks'

reactions before you decide Ricky's making a fool of himself. If a lively conversation about a former life as a king in Mesopotamia ensues, you're the one with hangups, not Ricky. Hassle him and you'll appear to be the party pooper.

3. *Try to prevent it*. If you're nervous about being totally humiliated for the rest of your life on account of partners like Ricky or Zelda, try to nip embarrassment in the bud. Without hostility or condescension, let your provocative partner know in advance what might bug you. She's more likely to respond well if you acknowledge that it is a free country and she can act any way she pleases, but . . .

"Ricky, the people at the bridge club are very straight, so could you cool it with the past-lives stuff unless someone brings it up?"

"Zelda, I don't want people to get the wrong impression of you tonight, so please don't fall all over my friends, OK?"

4. *Just watch and blush*. Remember that not every one of *your* social traits makes you Prince or Princess Charming. It may feel like agony, but you won't die from embarrassment.

FRIENDS, DATES, AND FAMILY

How do I know if someone I'm attracted to is attracted to me?

You'll know when your soon-to-be-sweetheart locks her gaze on yours with laserlike intensity. You stride to each other's side, forgetting time, place, and the people around you. In unison you murmur, "Finally we've found each other." Then it's wedding bells. Congratulations!

Fortunately, you can also know from much more subtle signals. Human beings do show they care with certain predictable pointers.

Attraction reactions

1. *Does she look at you more than she looks at other people and things?* Does she return your gaze and maybe add a smile when you look her way? Nine out of ten times, the person someone looks at most in a group is the one she'd like to impress. So if she keeps her head buried in the corn chips when you ask her opinion of your bold new tie, the odds are against you.

2. *Does he seem to be nervous when looking at you?* Does he startle when you look his way, and quickly shift his attention to those corn chips? This is the one-out-

95

of-ten guy who doesn't reciprocate your glances or indulge in more frequent looks at you when he feels attracted. Usually shy, or afraid to seem too eager, this guy acts as if you're dangerous stuff because inside he's quaking with his interest in you.

3. *Does she continue your conversation, even the small talk?* Most of us are too civilized to sniff each other out the way animals do. We let our voices explore for us. If she answers your questions, makes comments and, even better, asks you something about yourself, you're off to a great start.

4. *Does he listen, really listen?* Attentive listening indicates that he wants the interaction to continue. Watch for head nods, few interruptions, and encouragement to keep talking. If he acts as if you're Einstein when you're just describing your old convertible, he's hooked.

5. *Does she adjust to you nonverbally during conversation?* The more you like someone, the more you unconsciously adapt your body position and way of moving and talking to his. One researcher observed this pattern repeatedly among people attracted to each other in singles bars. When Mary sipped her drink, John did likewise. When John tapped to an easy listening tune, Mary's foot began to move with the rhythm of the music too.

Common attraction adaptions include:

- lowering or raising voice volume to match yours
- speeding up or slowing down to correspond to your pace of speaking
- shifting posture to parallel yours
- sitting down if you're sitting down

- standing up if you're standing up
- making similar gestures or movements
- laughing in unison
- breathing in unison

Sorry, you're not the one if—

- He talks about all the people at the party he wants to meet.
- You're doing your best Lily Tomlin routine and he's still futzing with the corn chips.
- He longingly watches a lively conversation ten feet away.
- He looks like he's about to sprint.
- He moves behind a potted tree when you try to gaze into his eyes.

I'm always awkward asking someone for a date.

Timid teenagers and sixty-something folks have a lot in common here. Even those of us who feel sure about our desirability obsess about how to get her to say yes and keep our cool if she says no. Stomachaches, heart flutters, and feelings of panic can accompany the risk of putting ourselves on the line. The term "dating phobia" is not too strong for those of us who'd rather suffer being alone than face the chance of being rebuffed.

Help begins in your head. Confident instigators share three basic attitudes. First, they think the reward is worth the risk. Second, they accept that they won't always be accepted. Third, they know that a no doesn't mean they're an undesirable creep that no one, anywhere, would want to spend time with.

Maxwell, a buddy from high school, has been an inspiration for my clients who fear taking the first step. An average-looking guy with above-average persistence, he'd call girl after girl, as many as twenty in a row sometimes, to get a date for the movies. He'd calmly cross each name off his list when he heard no. Feeling sad observing him dial his seventeenth try one day, I asked Maxwell, "How can you take it, girl after girl saying 'forget it'?" "Easy," he said. "I may get a lot of no's, but all it takes is one yes." Sure enough, he's now contentedly settled down with two teenagers who no doubt will carry on with Maxwell's Maxim.

Maxwell's Maxim for Persistence:
All It Takes Is One Yes.

To overcome asking-out awkwardness:

1. *Change your focus*. Reward yourself just for initiating, not for how many dates you succeed in getting. Start easily by asking out safe bets—people who've shown an interest in you or people who you aren't obsessed with—yet.

2. *See asking people out as a numbers game*. When you're job hunting, you don't expect every interviewer to go gaga. When you run a race, you know you won't win every time. Initiate as often as you can and lower your expectations. Not to sound cold about romance, but an acceptance rate of 10 percent—one out of every ten people you ask out says yes—can produce quite an enjoyable social life. At least according to my expert, Maxwell.

Note: You're entitled to pay some attention to your pride. If the same person refuses you twice, call it quits or you become a pest.

3. *Choose an initiation technique that feels comfortable to you*.
   • The traditional approach. Say something positive about your compatibility and suggest a possible date.
   "It's been fun to meet someone with as wacky a sense of humor as I have. Would you like to go to a comedy club next weekend?"
   (For a blind date) "Pamela thought we'd have a good time together. I'm wondering if you'd like to meet for coffee. There's a new Italian cafe on Beacon Street that's supposed to be good."
   • The compliment approach. Offer a sincere compliment and tie it in with your request for a date.
   "Your comments on movies are so astute. Would

99

you be interested in checking out the Hepburn retrospective this weekend?"

• The humble-me approach. Act as if you don't expect her to accept, but it sure would be great. This can flatter your prospective date and make her feel special. Exaggerate a little and you might charm her into a "shucks, yes."

"I'm sure you're booked from now until 1999, but I was wondering if you have three minutes sometime to get ice cream with me."

"Maybe you're only into million-dollar spreadsheets, but I have Dodgers tickets for next Tuesday."

• The ball-is-in-your-court approach. You express your interest but give him control of followup. Remember that you won't always get the response you're hoping for.

"What do you think about our having lunch together someday?"

"Would you be interested in seeing a movie some time?"

Or, if you feel gutsy like my friend Fast Eddie,

"When would you like to get together?"

I get nervous talking
to the opposite sex.

Talking to someone we're attracted to puts us smack into a stress-inducing situation. After all, we want to impress, we know we'll be sized up and the potential for rejection is real. Curiously, many of the physical signs of stress, like a rapid heart rate, changes in breathing, dizziness, and feeling too choked to speak also show up when we fall in love. So by feeling nervous you may be off to a promising start.

Seriously, a certain amount of stress may bring out your charm, energy, and breathless attention. Too large a dose, though, will feel dangerous. David felt comfortable having lunch with Dolores at work, but got into a tizzy before a Saturday evening concert she had asked him to. The idea of dating Dolores, who he'd never dreamed could think of him as anything more than a work friend, made butterflies in his stomach turn cartwheels. He considered canceling the date and his potential for a mate, he said, "if this is the kind of torture that lies ahead."

Help for the flutters

1. *Respect your reaction*. You're not nuts. It's normal to be sensitive about your lovability and concerned about how a conversation or date will go. However, you may be building up expectations or fantasies that feed your frenzy. Take your pulse on these unhelpful thoughts.

- *I know she's the one*. When all you've shared so far is small talk in line at the grocery store?
- *I know he won't like me*. Whoooaaa, you just met. Besides, if he doesn't respond you can still sur-

101

vive with dignity. In fact, everyone gets rejected some time or other and even Elizabeth Taylor doesn't get her man 100 percent of the time.

• *I'll make a fool of myself. She will know I'm nervous.* First, you do have control over how you act. Secondly, nervousness can be endearing to some. Think of Bob Newhart and Goldie Hawn.

David recognized that he was worried he'd disappoint Dolores once she got to know him outside of work. He reminded himself that all relationships involve learning about the other person's weak spots, that he'd find Dolores less than ideal eventually and that if she did end up dumping him it would hurt, but he would survive.

2. *Build up your scariness stamina.* Don't begin with the most formidable opposite-sex situations and then feel badly that you didn't cope or come across well. Keep in mind that avoiding situations provides short-term relief but long-term grief. To fortify your nerves, work your way up the following typical ladder of actions or create your own.

• saying hello to a person of the opposite sex
• initiating conversation
• making a phone call just to talk
• asking for a casual meeting (for coffee or a drink)
• asking for a date
• initiating and maintaining conversation on a date
• initiating handholding, then a kiss, and . . .

David decided he needed more comfort in after-work situations with Dolores before he felt ready for a Saturday-night date. He gave an excuse about the concert invitation but suggested they meet after work for dinner instead.

Before their dinner, he visualized himself coping well—and he did.

3. *Exercise physical control.* Though you may never find a cross-sex encounter as relaxing as a day at the beach, you can learn to manage your discomfort. Here are some techniques to consider.

• Deep and relaxed breathing. Irregular breathing is one of the easiest stress symptoms to control. With a hand on your abdomen, allow your belly to expand as you inhale and fall as you exhale. Let each inhalation and exhalation last for a count of three. Then count "Calm, two, three" silently as you breathe.

Along with his visualization of successful coping, David practiced relaxed breathing for several days before the big event. The result: more comfort, no indigestion, and conversation similar to what they usually enjoyed over lunch.

• Invisible tension. Squeeze together your thumb and middle finger—hard—before or during your stressful situation. In doing this, you channel and release tension in a way you can control.

• Healthy habits. Caffeine and nicotine exacerbate a stress reaction in many people. Though alcohol may appear to loosen you up, socially nervous people are more vulnerable to alcohol addiction. A physical workout does a healthier job of reducing uptightness.

• Poised stance. Carry yourself in a way that signals confidence. Often you come to feel the way you act, and your potential soul mate won't pick up as many signs of nervousness.

Note: If physical symptoms are overwhelming, seek a professional who specializes in stress reduction and working with social fears.

People say I come on too strong.

If you often get static back from dates, you may need to turn down the intensity of your transmission. People like to be wooed, not overwhelmed. You need to show enough interest to stimulate hers, but not so much that she's gasping for air.

Bob came to see me when Holly, a woman he was positive was "the one," told him bluntly to back off. When I asked Bob what had provoked her, he said he'd used a version of a Woody Allen line rather unsuccessfully. Over their first ice cream cone, Bob had confessed to Holly, "I'd like to be the father of your children."

Like Holly, most singles prefer subtlety. When six hundred college students rated opening lines for effectiveness, the winner was this modest-me approach: "I feel a little embarrassed but I'd like to meet you." Near the bottom of the list was the brazen, "Your place or mine?"

You're just too much if you do or say the following:

- Tell him he's the *most* anything (handsome, creative, funny) you've ever met when you've just met.
- Keep your gaze fixed on her face like crazy glue, when she's eyeing others in the crowd as well.
- Wonder aloud if he has any secret tattoos before you've even held hands.
- Bring up the benefits of filing taxes jointly before you and she have even negotiated splitting a restaurant tab.
- Initiate dates, phone calls, conversations three times more often than he reciprocates.
- Send roses and caramels while she's sending messages like

"We just met"

"Whoa!"

"Let's take it one step at a time"

"You're moving too fast"

"Hey, bud, are you the one who keeps sending me flowers?"

Tone it down to have connections last longer

1. *Cut the premature intimacy*. Except for those rare occurrences where you truly lock eyes and lives à la Romeo and Juliet, most relationships take time to grow. Don't talk about how the two of you were meant to be when you haven't been or done much of anything yet.

Bob would have impressed Holly more with a dialogue about favorite ice cream flavors than his desire to father her family.

2. *Space out*. She needs space—literally—to decide whether she wants to get closer to you. Keep a distance physically of a foot or more, and let her be the one to inch closer. Holly felt uncomfortable when Bob veered in to take a lick of her ice cream cone.

3. *Water it down*. If you're interested in personal talk, keep the focus on yourself, not the relationship, at first.

DON'T SAY: "Let's go to that outdoor concert series this summer."

TRY: "I really enjoy outdoor concerts."

Ask open questions so he won't feel trapped or embarrassed.

DON'T SAY: "Are you interested in a committed relationship?"

TRY: "So what kind of relationship are you looking for eventually?"

Compliments are fine but make them specific, not idealistic.

DON'T SAY: "I can't stop staring into your eyes."

TRY: "You've got wonderful green eyes."

Question softeners can also make her more comfortable when the time comes to discuss the two of you.

"You don't have to answer this, but how do you think we get along?"

"I hope you won't feel on the spot—I'm wondering if you like me as much as I like you."

"There's something I hope you won't mind me asking. Do you think we should continue going out?"

How do I find out if someone is married or unattached?

Zack wasn't shy so much as bumbling when it came to asking women out. On striking up an exceptional rapport with a woman, he had a tendency to blurt out the first thing that came to mind—with less than happy results. Once after chatting on and on with a consultant he'd hired to computerize his customer list, he touched her arm and said, "Susan, I really like you a lot. Would you have dinner with me Friday night?" Susan blushed, gave him a strange, long look and then replied, "I think we ought to keep this on a professional level." Weeks later, he learned that Susan was married, and he blushed, for having put both of them in an awkward position. To prevent a recurrence, Zack decided he would try to determine first whether or not a woman was attached. But how?

Snooping about someone's availability status

1. *Get an intermediary to help*. Dispatch a socially skilled friend on the mission of finding out whether Mr. or Ms. Mystery is a candidate for dates or a relationship. Of course you may need to watch out if your friend is especially appealing. At a conference Zack attended with his buddy Ed, he sent Ed to check out a woman who'd sent him smiles across an auditorium aisle earlier in the day. About ten minutes later, Ed beckoned him over and introduced him to Priscilla, who said hello to Zack, then focused her attention back on Ed. Poor Zack! Priscilla *was* available, but Ed charmed her first.

2. *Play "I Spy."* Follow the mystery person home and check the names on the mailbox. Call his home number

and listen for clues in the answering-machine message. Pretend to be doing a phone survey: "Would you like to be on our lunch dates mailing list?" Or call the person's home and ask to speak to "Mrs. _____ " or ask, "May I speak to your husband?"

3. *Ask indirectly*. During conversation, make reference to your prospect's "mate." She'll probably correct you if she's unattached.

You: "I guess you and your husband take advantage of living so near ski slopes."

She: "*I* do, but I don't have a husband."

Or, bring up the topic of attached and unattached folks. Chances are he'll drop a revealing hint in response.

You: "Dancing classes seem more fun if you have a steady partner to go with. I don't know how comfortable I'd feel taking them as a single."

He: "I know what you mean. When I was single, I even disliked going to the movies alone."

4. *Ask directly*. There's nothing wrong with being up-front so both of you know the limits of where things might be headed.

"I'd love to get to know you better. Do you mind if I ask if you're attached?"

"I don't want to come on too strong, but I'm wondering, are you married?"

And, for the more bold among you:

"So, is there any hope for us going out?"

"Tell me you're not attached and I'll be thrilled."

How do I get a shy person of the opposite sex to open up?

It shouldn't be difficult for you to understand how it feels to be shy. According to Stanford University psychologist Philip Zimbardo, 80 percent of the people in one study revealed that they had experienced shyness at one time or another in their lives. Harvard University researcher Jerome Kagan has found that 10 to 20 percent of the population, those who are "temperamentally shy," have had intense physical and emotional responses to new people and situations from a very young age. These folks habitually freeze in the face of social stress, unable to interact smoothly.

Keep in mind that for the shy, nothing is more nerve-racking than an initial encounter with the opposite sex. In fact, the greater the attraction, the stronger the shy reaction. Ruby smiled at Hal every day at the French bakery cafe where they both regularly lunched. Hal would give Ruby a quick glance and then nervously bend over his calculator and punch numbers. Ruby wanted to chat but sensed that even an attempt at small talk would spook him. Will she ever make Hal a pal? There's hope if she knows how to respect the reticent.

Ten tips for reaching the reserved

1. Come on slow, not strong.
2. Be warm, not hot. Gush makes her blush.
3. Stay on your side of the table. Don't touch!
4. Talk more about yourself at first.
5. Ask easy questions for starters.

Try "Do you work around here?" not, "Do you agree with the view of the world expressed in Dante's *Inferno?*"

6. Look for subtle signs of interest—a slight smile, a quick head turn your way, an answer of more than two syllables.

7. Understand that shyness isn't snobbiness. Though they find it difficult to respond, shy people usually do appreciate your show of interest and efforts to get to know them.

8. Don't comment on her shyness, or on her demeanor at all. She's extremely concerned about people's impressions and will want to die if people call her shy.

9. Disclose your own feelings. Talk about a hangup or two of yours to see if you get a response.

   "Being from a small town, I sometimes have trouble keeping up with the city pace."

10. Ask for advice. This may get the shy guy out of his shell and into you.

    "Do you know any good exotic restaurants in this neighborhood?"

OK, one more!

11. If she's shy, give it one more try. Usually I say give a person three chances to engage in conversation with you, and if you get only grunts or monosyllables, move on. But if you're sweet on her and convinced it's shyness rather than lack of interest, stick around.

Everyone likes me — as a friend.

Marty, a decent-looking twenty-nine-year-old man, had had it with his lifelong role as girls' "best friend." Women enjoyed his good advice and listening, but he often wished they wanted more. All the more frustrating, his female friends paired off with guys he considered "less qualified" for a relationship. Marty liked being liked, but he wanted to inspire romance as well.

Fortunately or unfortunately, researchers haven't unmasked all the mysteries of human sexual attraction. A person's idea of good looks, the partner's mood at meeting, smell, sound, touch, and reminding another of someone else all too often enter into the equation. But whether you come across as a potential paramour or just a pal can depend on your skill in delivering the "flirt factor."

Four ways to ignite romance

1. *Come alive*. People are attracted to those whose faces move and change while listening and speaking. Warming up a frozen or deadpan look with expression will make gazing at you a more pleasurable experience. Changes in the pitch and volume of your voice, as opposed to using a monotone, help too. Practice in front of a mirror at home if you need to.

2. *Attune*. You're on her wavelength to the extent that your gestures, facial expressions, and body postures match hers. You shouldn't ape someone you're interested in ("Let's see. She just lifted her pinky at a 15-degree angle. I'll go get my protractor and do the same") so much as monitor yourself to make sure you're not so different she'll think you two would never click. (See "How do I

111

know if someone I'm attracted to is attracted to me?" [p. 95] for parallel behaviors that signal interest.)

3. *Make contact but hold a little back*. Smile, and don't just turn up your mouth. Let your whole face, especially your eyes, show warmth. Ask questions and pay attention to the answers. Sit closer than you normally would, lean in and touch—fleetingly and in a neutral zone such as a hand, an arm, or a shoulder. Show interest without coming on too strong. Allow pauses so that he can volley back with a question to you. Look away, instigating him to try to gain your attention again. Remember that many people gravitate to someone who's a mystery, so control your urge for total instant connection.

Women enjoyed relating to Marty because he kept the conversation rolling and showed unfailing interest in what the woman was thinking and feeling. But we agreed he needed to cool his involvement a bit to get her temperature rising.

4. *Show you care*. Marty asked women that he worked with why so many of them blushed when Julio, an average-looking guy so far as he could see, walked by their desks and said hello. He learned that Julio set hearts throbbing because he had a way of offering unexpected compliments. Marty needed to master this and other conversational tactics that make someone feel special.

• Compliment: Mention something that catches your attention in his appearance, attitude, or conversation.

"I love outrageous ties. I bet you're a creative person."

"You seem enthusiastic about your work. So many people aren't."

112

"You're the first person I've met in a long time who hasn't asked my occupation in the first two minutes."

• Be careful, especially in work situations, to avoid compliments that could be considered sexual, such as, "Your legs look really nice today."

• Remember details: She'll feel flattered when you ask about and refer later to things that are important to her. My husband impressed me on our second date when he remembered my nieces' names, not to mention the names of their dolls he'd seen in a picture. Marty talked politics with women easily, but when he learned to find out when she walked her dog or the history of each of her rings, he got a fluttery response that women hadn't given him before.

• Ask his opinion: People feel special when you single them out for advice, especially on matters they don't discuss with the average person.

"What do you think of this color shirt on me?"

"Do you think I should go to Club Med or on a cruise for my vacation?"

• Reveal feelings—carefully: Don't suddenly spring on her that she's the love of your life, just provide subtle feedback that there's potential. Drop a phrase or two about how you feel.

"I had a great time this afternoon."

"Talking to you is always fun."

"It's great to meet someone who shares my values."

"I'd love to give you a hug."

• Create fun: A big part of flirting is an atmosphere of fun. If you've had a successful meeting or two, follow up in an amusing way. Sample ideas: photocopy your lips and sign them, call him to share a joke you heard, or send a valentine in August.

I seem to do all the work in conversation.

If this occurs at the beginning of a relationship, your greater effort may signify that you're more interested, since lack of response is a common way of trying to communicate "forget it." If this characteristically occurs in all your conversations or over time with one specific person, you have what is known as an unbalanced talk/listen ratio. Either you dominate to the degree that she can't get a word in edgewise or you've found a conversational partner who is lazy or too good a listener. As a conversational burden bearer, you may come across as self-centered and a poor listener. In contrast, the most satisfying relationships involve a balance over several conversational sessions in time spent talking and listening.

Once positive rapport is established, gender factors often come into play. Contrary to popular belief, women are not the gabbier sex. Not only do men talk more and at greater length, women usually let them go on without much interruption. Talkative men may bemoan the fact that a woman doesn't have much to say, but in her mind, she doesn't feel like fighting for the floor.

In intimate relationships, women more often perform the work of conversational maintenance. To keep the conversational game in motion, they use attention getters like "Hey, did you hear about . . . ?" and ask about five times as many questions as men. Women hope this work has a payoff, that the conversation establishes a closer connection.

If you're drained from working overtime in conversation, you need time out to relax and refresh. By taking it easy for a while, you'll be on your way to a more restful conversational style.

Taking a conversational vacation

1. *Scout the territory*. Observe your conversations for patterns that occur with the opposite sex. Look for these common causes of unbalance.

Men's work:

- doing all the initiating early in the relationship
- having to appear the expert by talking at length
- having to entertain through humor and stories

Women's work:

- one-sidedly revealing and seeking personal information early in the relationship
- making frequent overtures to persuade him to talk
- putting energy into what he wants to talk about while sacrificing topics important to you

2. *Quit working and rest more during conversation*. Since you take good conversations as your responsibility, you don't allow your counterpart to pull her weight. Trust that neither the conversation nor the world will fall apart if you do less. Cut back on the following behaviors by half:

- initiating topics
- asking questions
- jumping in or picking up the pace if there's silence
- responding at great length

3. *Now slow down and drop out*. Try letting go altogether of at least one part of your conversational work load. When you work less, talking partners tend to take up the slack and work more. Some ideas:

• Don't begin a new topic or ask a question after a silence. He probably will eventually. Allow fifteen full seconds—an excruciatingly long pause to many people—before you speak up.

• Pause more after comments and questions. Her pace may differ from yours, so that she needs more time to jump in.

• Watch the clock. Literally place yourself in sight of a clock and talk for no longer than thirty to forty-five seconds each conversational turn.

I'd like to be a more interesting conversationalist on dates.

Though even the most meaningful dialogue won't compensate for a lack of chemistry, a meeting of minds and voices can't hurt. Garth had plenty of friends of both sexes and could chat away comfortably during long lunches and dinners. Yet in a dating situation, Garth monitored every word out of his mouth, concerned he'd sound dumb or silly. He spent so much time watering down his conversation that he accurately described himself as a dull date. Like many of us, Garth needed a brushup in tête-à-tête fundamentals.

For conversational charisma on command—

1. *Make her feel marvelous.* The best conversationalists are known for being avid listeners and making their conversational partner feel good. In saying good-bye to Johnny Carson after twenty-nine years on TV, here's how his famous guests described his charm:

"He gets things out of you that make you seem clever."—Tony Randall

"He's a kind interviewer and he makes his guests look good."—Morgan Fairchild

"Being with Carson is like being with someone who is terrific in bed."—Mariette Hartley

2. *Be stimulating, not dull.* Keep your conversational computer full of interesting items to talk about. Here's how.

- Keep up with current events and issues—and take a stand on controversial matters.

• Learn more about the other half—consider a subscription to popular magazines geared to the opposite sex.

• Consider a little show and tell—carry a conversation piece like an autograph of your favorite singer or a valuable old coin to get his attention in a fun way.

3. *Be a flexible communicator.* The best conversationalists aren't one-note people. Conversational mood can run from rhetorical to ridiculous, and topics from emotional to abstract. Talented talkers are unpredictable, and unlike Garth, not too concerned about playing it safe. These stretchers add dimension to conversations:

• Share experiences. Tell personal stories and anecdotes, the funnier, more frightening, or weirder the better. How about the time you searched the town dump to find the winning lottery ticket you'd tossed away? When you practice your tales on a friend at work before trying them out on dates, you're likely to put the punchlines and pauses in the right places.

• Express your point of view. You'll be more interesting to the extent that you define your distinct personality by saying, "I feel . . . ," "I believe . . . ," "I don't agree with . . ." in discussions rather than going along for the sake of being nice. When asked what attracted them to their mates, people usually say, "He was different," not "She was the same as everyone else." Note: It's a turnoff if you're too opinionated—meaning that you don't acknowledge his right to believe differently.

• Show different sides of yourself. In the course of dating, make sure you express the range of your personality. Garth realized he was toning down the wild and crazy impulses his friends were fond of for lukewarm likability. Once he invited a new date out for a walk in the rain, he knew he was on his way to revealing his sillier side.

Are you showing your best sides? Circle five of the following traits that you'd like a date to see. Think back to your last date and recall which sides you actually showed in your interaction. Set a goal for another side you may want to express next time.

analytical
bubbly
clever
confident
creative
expert
flexible
forceful
fun-loving
funny
goal-oriented
helpful
intuitive
knowledgeable
light-hearted
mellow
mysterious

observant
persuasive
philosophical
quirky
self-effacing
serious
spiritual
spontaneous
strong-willed
successful
sympathetic
tactful
thoughtful
tolerant
vulnerable
witty

How can I clearly set sexual limits on a date?

Ellen invited Bruce in after a fun night belting out songs at a karaoke bar. She wanted to get to know Bruce better and figure out if she was attracted to him. She told him —and this was true—that she wanted to try out her new cappuccino maker. Bruce, who had the hots for Ellen, felt relieved that she wasn't playing hard to get and checked his wallet to make sure he had protection with him.

Misinterpreting sexual signals in the dating game is common. No one sex is at fault, but both sexes need to be up front and rely less on reading between the lines before jumping between the sheets. Like Bruce, men may interpret innocent interactions as sexual invitations, because of wishful thinking or a sincere belief that women generally come on indirectly. One study of college males indicated that 30 percent did not believe a woman means no when she says no.

For their part, women may expect to be taken literally (a cappuccino is a cappuccino, not an invitation to stay until breakfast) or may be oblivious to male intentions. Not wanting to offend, some women feel uncomfortable speaking up and setting limits, especially with someone whose affection they may want. The downside to playing it by ear is that when you don't sing out, it is impossible to know what tune your date may be hearing.

The good news is that most sexual misunderstandings get negotiated, and that communication can serve as a tool to set your boundaries in this most sensitive area. Whether you ever become sexual partners or not, it's important that you go all the way when:

Speaking up about sexual limits

1. *Language counts.* Your goal is stating your limits without offending or apologizing. Choose the tune you're most comfortable with.

- He's so fine, but . . .
  "Bruce, I really like you, but tonight let's stick with holding hands at the kitchen table."
- Stop in the name of love.
  "Bridget, I'm not ready to get involved physically till we know each other better."
  "I think we should wait and see how things evolve."
- Just one look, or . . .
  "I feel comfortable with just hugging or napping together, but nothing more sexual."
  "A massage would be great but I don't want to make love."
- We can work it out.
  "Let's talk about where we both stand regarding making love."
  "I think we need to take things more slowly. What do you think?"
- Will you still love me tomorrow?
  "I hope this doesn't offend you, Bruce, but I never do anything more than kiss on a second date."
  "I don't want to hurt your feelings, Bridget, but let's save this for when we know each other better."
- Hey you, get off of my . . .
  Sometimes you need some direct statements to redirect your date.
  "Bridget, would you please take your hands out of my pockets?"
  "Bruce, my clothes stay on. More coffee?"

2. *Timing counts*. Since the best time to be clear is sooner, not later, it's best to make up your mind either beforehand or early in the date how far you want to take things. Some optimal moments:

• At the first invitation to be alone. Although Bruce may consider Ellen paranoid if she says, "I *only* want to talk and have cappuccino" (Bruce's reply: "What did you think I would do, jump on your bones?"), still, chances are he won't be taking out his wallet for a condom check.

• At the first touch. Be explicit at the first kiss or hug. No matter how far you've gone, though, you can still state limits. When she's getting out the whipped cream and running the bath, you still have the right to say forget it.

I'm embarrassed bringing up the subject of condoms.

Most communication situations are not life or death matters, but this one is. Rationally, most of us would choose embarrassment over a dread disease. As one single female put it, "Better red than dead." When a lustful moment looms, however, we worry that we'll ruin the mood by sounding clinical. Or we presume that our partner will display the requisite savoir faire an instant before it's too late. Though prophylactics aren't the stuff of love poems, no subject matters more when your communication gets really close.

Safe talk (How to handle condom conversation)

1. *Prophylactically speaking.* Prevent a problem with condoms by bringing up the subject way before you'll need to use them. Drop a hint about what you expect by referring to the importance of condoms in general. With the following tactics, only a blockhead would miss your point.

- The "I-read-something" approach. "I read that most sexually active teenagers aren't using condoms. That's like playing Russian Roulette."
- The "I-know-someone" approach. "I have a friend who refuses to use condoms and I'm not surprised no one wants to get serious with him."
- The "I'm-the-type-of-person" approach. "I'm the type of person who's committed to good health, from running every day to caring about safe sex."

2. *Does he or doesn't he?* A woman who assumes that an educated man knows about safe sex may avoid finding

out his condom I.Q. Bad move—he may be more comfortable reading Kafka than rolling on some protection. Others find themselves in the midst of an amorous entanglement leaving protection to chance. Get in control by broaching the subject or bringing out the condom. If you're shy, you might want to have a line ready that you feel comfortable with. Some lines to try on:

"This is awkward, but we need to talk about protection."

"I'll be more relaxed if I know that you have a condom."

"Let's decide what to do for safe sex."

"Your condom or mine?"

"Where is it? No, I mean the condom."

3. *Does she or doesn't she?* Men, don't assume she has X-ray vision into your wallet or dresser drawer. Let her know she'll be safe with you, or that you're out of provisions. Some wrapper openers:

"Here it is—my trusty foiled friend."

"Just to let you know, I'll use a condom when the time comes."

"Would you like to choose from my condom collection?"

"I flunked Boy Scouts—are you prepared?"

"I hate to ask, but do you have something latex nearby?"

4. *Caught without a condom.* If neither of you is prepared, be ready to say no to less than safe sex.

"Too bad, but it's out of bed and over to the drugstore."

"I just can't feel comfortable if we don't use something."

"It's not a good idea for us to do something we'll later regret."

"How about if we just neck this time?"

I'm not up for romance — but I don't want to hurt her.

Since rejection by the opposite sex tops everyone's lists of sore spots, it's best to learn how to communicate "buzz off" without heartbreaking bluntness. If you're apt to play along because you can't bear to hurt, both of you are losing out—you because you know it's going nowhere, he because he could be getting somewhere with someone else.

Cliff decided that any relationship with Mandy was doomed the minute he sneezed on her when she pecked him on the cheek after they had coffee together one evening. He took it as proof of what he'd already sensed—that he just wasn't interested. Terrified, though, to douse her hopes when she left a message on his answering machine inviting him to the movies, Cliff tried the easy way out by not calling her for a week. No luck. Mandy woke him up Saturday morning to coo that she was in the middle of making omelets for two. Cliff did like Mandy as a friend, but needed to learn:

How to say "You're not that special person."

1. *Keep your physical distance when together.* Mandy would have smelled trouble if she clutched Cliff's arm in the cafe and he said, "Ouch."

2. *Accept only occasional invites and don't initiate until the relationship settles into something less than she wants it to be.*

3. *Try the independent/unavailable/messed up excuse.* This way you accept responsibility for the relation-

125

ship not working instead of mentioning why you don't click.

"I'm at a stage where I need a lot of elbow room."

"I'm still getting over my divorce and won't be ready to get involved for a while."

"I'm not together enough to handle a relationship right now."

4. *If she still wants to woo you out of your solo existence, be more direct.* Focus on compatibility differences rather than lack of attraction.

DON'T SAY: "You're much too lazy for me."
TRY: "We live at such different paces, it's a strain to get together."

DON'T SAY: "Your body is a major turnoff."
TRY: "I'm looking for someone who's into kayaking every weekend."

DON'T SAY: "I have a fantastic urge to nap whenever we go out."
TRY: "I don't think we have much in common."

5. *If you've tried all that and he's still falling fast, come right out with the truth:*
"I'm sorry, but I really can't see us as a couple."

"Going out doesn't feel right to me."

"I'm not into dating you, but I've loved our discussions of Elvis."

How can I break up gracefully with someone?

Tim did not like taking second place to skiing in Beth's life. After spending hours waiting for her in the ski lodge two weekends in a row, he knew their sports incompatibility put the relationship on a real downward slope. Preoccupied with bigger and better mountains, Beth had no idea her relationship with Tim was slipping fast. Tim wanted to get up the courage to call it quits but, afraid of hurting Beth's feelings, he froze.

Though being the breaker-upper feels like a bad-guy role, in the long run you're both better off to free yourselves for other liaisons. Although you can't prevent hurt feelings, remember that if only one party cares to be in it, a relationship won't work.

Making breaking up less hard to do

Once you're convinced that it's best to split up, you can be a lot kinder than telling her to take a flying leap off a slippery slope. Use one of the following strategies.

1. *The wind down*. Here you hint that something's changed by being less available, not calling as much, and talking more about matters outside the relationship. Your goal is to have him take stock of these changes and initiate discussion of what's going on. This approach helps align your behavior with your feelings, though critics may call it cowardly or manipulative.

2. *The open discussion*. In this approach you launch a discussion of how the relationship is going, so your soon-to-be-ex paramour participates equally in making deci-

sions about the future. Here you're hoping she'll hear the difference in your feelings for each other and realize a breakup is for the best. Some starters:

"Beth, how do you think our relationship has been lately?"

"I think we should talk about how things are going with us."

"Let's talk about the kind of relationship we each want."

3. *The get-it-over-quickly approach*. If you've made up your mind and want to get out, you want to be clear without causing unnecessary hurt. You're not initiating discussion so much as announcing where you are headed. This works best if you're dealing with someone who's been oblivious to what's been happening or if your feelings are so limited you'd rather not dissect a relationship that hardly existed.

"You know, given your preoccupation with skiing and mine with computers, I think we're better off as friends."

"Beth, I've been thinking a lot lately. I really don't think we're all that compatible and I think it would be best if we didn't go out any more."

Can I really be friends with someone of the opposite sex?

Both sexes benefit from what researchers call mixed-sex friendships. Men open up and reveal more about themselves with women friends than with other males, perhaps because there's less of an atmosphere of competition. Though women are not necessarily more open with men, they find talking with male friends helpful for other reasons. Melanie's friend Buff helps her through the hard times in her dating relationships because he provides a male perspective without the emotional entanglement. Buff has illuminated one fellow's obsession with football and another's reluctance to split the dinner check with her. Melanie also appreciates Buff's decisiveness (about everything from where to eat to why the death penalty is discriminatory) as a contrast to her best friend Rona's dilly-dallying, when a decision about what to have for dinner democratically drags on forever.

For mixed-sex friendships to thrive, one person can't be secretly longing for true love to blossom. Also, the friends' spouses or lovers must feel at ease with their special someone's spending time together with another man or woman. Though friendships ideally develop irrespective of gender and more out of trust and compatibility, friendship can take on noteworthy dimensions when we befriend the other half of the human race.

For close encounters of a different kind—

1. *Let it happen.* Many opposite-sex friendships emerge in the midst of sharing time and tasks at work or in voluntary organizations. In a study conducted at the University of Michigan, 22 percent of managers surveyed

experienced close relationships (with sexual feelings that were not acted on) with business colleagues. Incidentally, those involved in these opposite-sex friendships viewed them as beneficial to both the friends and the corporation.

2. *Be clear.* Who feels what toward whom may need to be explicit when you get friendly with someone of the opposite sex. If you're attached, feel further development of a relationship would be risky, or are not attracted to the person as a potential partner, fine—but don't assume he can read your mind. To clarify your intentions:

- Mention a significant other or desire to meet someone.
- Confide in her about a problem related to handling the above.
- Use the word "friend" a lot.
- Call attention to your wedding band, your engagement ring, or the pictures of your boyfriend or girlfriend on your desk.
- Avoid asking your friend to social events or date-night events at first.
- Don't use endearments or touch that could be misinterpreted.
- Go dutch—don't pay the bill.

See "I'm not up for romance but I don't want to hurt her" (p. 125) on what to do if your opposite number falsely assumes you're romantically interested.

3. *Don't expect "birds of a feather."* If you find a soul mate in your opposite-sex friend, terrific, but more likely you'll find differences in what you give and get from this friendship. Male/female role issues often emerge, for instance, even without intimacy. Buff instinctively took a protective stance when one of Melanie's dates didn't phone for a week ("I'd like to punch that guy out"). Mel-

anie couldn't stand it when Buff rated women's looks on a scale of one to five. Gender differences in communication that can affect friendships include:

- how much time you want to spend talking vs. doing an activity
- how much support or stroking you expect and want
- how you each give or accept advice
- how well you listen and how much you want to be listened to
- how you handle disagreements
- how you use language, slang, and curses
- how you talk about the other sex

At social gatherings men stick with men and women with women.

George and Diane were confident that the guests they'd invited to a party would mix well, since they all had teenaged kids and careers in the medical field. Yet the party, otherwise a success, had one twist George and Diane hadn't expected—voluntary sexual segregation. While the women warmed up the kitchen talking about how to keep their kids out of trouble, the men mingled in the den discussing whether or not it made sense to buy American.

Wondering whether their party represented a throwback to hunting-and-gathering-society roles, George and Diane asked me if they could do anything next time to encourage mingling. The factors that needed to be overcome, I pointed out, stemmed less from our ancestors in the jungle than preferences established and reinforced in our lifetimes.

The scoop on social sexual separation

1. *Preferred conversational topics differ by sex.* One survey of women and men aged seventeen to eighty-six reported that males were more likely than females to discuss music, the news, and sports, while females talked about relationships, family, health, weight, food, and clothing far more often than males. Sexual separation at parties thus reduces the yawn factor.

2. *The communication styles of men and women differ.* Men tend to enjoy contesting, arguing, and displaying knowledge and prowess and seek conversational partners who will do the same. Women tend to favor talking about people (including the guys in the other

room), supporting, listening, and exchanging personal stories.

3. *In mixed groups, men usually dominate and women don't like to feel left out.* Women may yield to men's strength in raising topics or gaining attention in groups. They do this to be polite—but may feel a lot more at ease at the coffee-klatsch.

4. *Men feel they have to be polite to a woman who speaks up in a party situation.* They may be more gallant about paying attention and refraining from interrupting (which feels especially difficult if she takes forever to get to the punchline). This forced adaptation makes the den seem a less demanding situation.

If, like George and Diane, you're determined despite those difficulties to host a gender-neutral party, consider these tips:

Socializing without separation by sex

1. *Keep the party in one room.* If one sex begins to migrate, let's say to the kitchen, assign a person of the opposite gender to bust up their fun.

2. *Plan gender-neutral activities, where the focus is on the event.* Trivia games, charades, Twister, square dancing, and volleyball work well. Theme parties, mystery parties, and costume parties also keep everyone content with mixed company.

3. *Play host helper.* Nudge interaction along by mentioning commonalities among seemingly alien beings.

"Fred, this is Joanne. Joanne also recently received funding for a public health education program."

4. *If these fail but guests are having fun, call it quits with your ambition to be a social engineer.* Keep in mind that people socialize to relax, not to practice for utopia.

I'm never sure if I should hug, shake hands, or kiss when greeting friends, relatives, or new acquaintances.

Each of us has a preferred greeting style shaped by our personality and how touchy our immediate family was with each other. Distant Doris feels well met with a hands-off hello, while Down-your-neck Don feels put off if he receives less than a full-body hug. In addition, different groups, whether a family, a clique, or a geographical set, have customs governing the range of appropriate greetings. At a holistic healing convention, the norm may be for both sexes to hug strangers, while at an upper-crust charity board, women may characteristically brush cheeks and men nod at each other or extend hands to be shaken. In a setting where we feel at home, whatever we feel comfortable doing usually comes off fine. But we can flounder in a strange environment or among people who are touchier or more standoffish than we are. Though it's impossible to present every permutation of greeting etiquette, the following principles should help.

Greeting relatives and relative strangers

1. *Since more women are concerned about being touched by men than vice versa, it's best if a man defers to the woman's greeting style*. If she offers a peck on the cheek, don't send back a fat wet smooch.

2. *Defer to age and status too*. If Great Grandma Gertrude pinches your cheeks, suffer.

3. *If you're the guest, let the hosts set the tone*. In other words, when at the Romanoffs', do as the Romanoffs

do. Greetings don't last long. At most you'll have to endure ten seconds of feeling uncomfortable.

4. *When in doubt, hold off for a moment.* Although greetings do go by very fast, you can usually wait for a count of two to give the other person a chance to indicate or initiate a preference. Watch and be prepared to smoothly match the hand or cheek extended. Duane was eager to welcome the parents of his friend Kazuo, who had flown in from Tokyo for their son's business school graduation. In his nervousness, he rushed to crunch the hand of Mrs. Yoshikawa and gave Mr. Yoshikawa a slap on the side of the shoulder, which he found shockingly disrespectful. Had Duane paused, he would have been able to go along with the nod or bow that Kazuo's parents would have felt more comfortable with.

5. *It's better to come off as too reserved than to overwhelm the other person.* A genuine smile will help correct any impression of aloofness left by a greeting more distant than the other person was used to.

6. *Prepare some lines to use if you suspect you'll be confronted with expectations you know will make you intolerably uptight.* If you dread cousin Bernie's bear hugs for weeks before his son's bar mitzvah, if the memory of Boris kissing you—a man—on both cheeks makes you want to avoid seeing him again, you can assert control over the situation with words that take you off the hook. For example:

"Bernie, no hug for me today. It's my back. I paid a fortune to my chiropractor this week, and I still need to be careful."

"Boris, I hope you don't mind if I say hello American-style. Here." (Extend a hand.)

I'm a klutz at comforting someone of the opposite sex.

Both sexes are equally devastated by a loss, serious disease, or other life crisis. Yet the demeanor we display to the world when we're distressed and the types of comfort we appreciate from others may vary greatly. Wanting to offer comfort but not knowing how can be agonizing, especially when we feel close to someone.

Herb felt pained when he learned that his coworker, Margaret, had suffered a traumatic miscarriage over the weekend in her fourth month of pregnancy. Not sure how to broach the subject, though, he kept mum. When Margaret sadly asked, "Did you hear the bad news?" he was caught off guard and replied, "Oh, sure." Concerned that he had done the wrong thing, he sought out Margaret later that day to reassure her that this wasn't the end of the world and that things were certain to get better for her soon. Though Margaret understood Herb's good intentions, she couldn't bear his dismissal of a wound that was still so fresh for her.

Gender and grief: A primer

1. *Both sexes appreciate your initiating an expression of concern rather than avoiding the issue*. Herb thought that by mentioning the miscarriage, he'd upset Margaret too much, but that's rarely so. Do be sensitive to where and in whose presence you bring up a sad or private matter. For example, since Herb did not know who Margaret would and would not confide in, expressing sympathy would only have been appropriate when they were alone.

2. *Both sexes appreciate a simple expression of your concern initially*. Kind words such as these will mean a lot:

"I'm so sorry about . . ."

"I feel very sad for you . . ."

"I've been thinking about you."

A wordless hug, a note, flowers, or a treat left on a desk can also convey your compassion.

3. *Men sometimes want to solve a person's problems*. This would be nice, but you can't take away the pain. Especially avoid offering solutions or advice to women unless you're asked. They may hear comments like these as condescending and irrelevant to the current preoccupation, their pain:

"Have you considered adoption?"

"The clinic in my hometown is good at treating kids with leukemia. Would you like me to call them for you?"

"The police don't take shootings seriously any more. I know a good private detective you could hire to discover who killed your father."

4. *Some women give men in mourning an overdose of understanding*. Many men have a low tolerance for sympathy since it makes them feel powerless. A man in pain may be working on getting over it and recoil at what he takes as a woman's tendency to "wallow" in the situation. If you extend sympathy to a man and he says something like "Well, I'm just going to get on with my life," or "That's life," cool it with the condolences.

5. *Some men minimize a person's problems in order to reassure*. When men do this to each other, they understand the intention. But using this attempt at comfort with a woman puts you at risk of being considered insen-

sitive. Diminishing phrases like these may relieve your discomfort, but probably not hers:

"It could have been worse."

"At least you have two other kids."

"You'll get over it soon."

6. *Women often share similar stories with people in crisis as a way of saying "You're not alone."* Margaret found it comforting to hear of friends' and coworkers' traumatic pregnancy losses and felt a closer bond with them. Men should take care when they share a tragic story with a woman that it won't come across as "If you think you have problems, listen to this . . ."

7. *All human beings like to know you're there if they need you.* Just say, "Let me know if you want to talk or if there's any way I can be helpful."

You'll note that certain shoulders are easier to cry on over certain issues. It made sense that Margaret shared deeper feelings about her loss with her assistant, who had experienced a stillbirth the previous year.

I don't want to be approached so much by the opposite sex.

Short of keeping your hair greasy or wearing garlic around your neck, there's no magic that keeps members of the opposite sex at bay when you prefer to be alone. But if you're bothered because you can't open a book on a park bench without conversation pursuers distracting you, you can gain control by monitoring the signals you're giving off and your responses when someone intrudes on you with talk.

To remain alone, stop sending hints that are likely to be interpreted as "Please approach me." Greg, a friendly engineer who often appeared frumpled and lost, seemed to attract as much attention from women as a vulnerable little puppy. Disturbed about his irresistible attractiveness to other women, his fiancée advised that he look less open by erasing his perpetual grin and that he move from place to place more purposefully. Andie was offended that men seemed overly interested in her, but her habit of tossing her long hair while sizing up everyone in the vicinity ranked high on the list of women's availability signals. When she saved her hair tossing for the times she wanted to meet someone, her complaints diminished.

In choosing a send-off strategy, be sensitive to the risk that your pursuer took in approaching you. So unless he's rude, raunchy, or really obnoxious, try to spare feelings as you fend him off. You'll feel better for handling the brushoff in a friendly manner. Whenever she doesn't get the hint, of course your good-bye signals will have to become stronger.

Getting rid of someone without being rude

1. *The happy hint*. While being as friendly as you like, make prominent mention of a mate or relationship that makes you unavailable. Remember that if you really are out of the courtship game, your suitor will probably want to know right away too.

Pursuer: So do you live around here?
You: We just moved into a complex.
Her: What do you do?
You: My girlfriend and I have a jewelry repair business.
Her: Oh that's nice . . .

2. *The brief response*. Here you provide minimally informative responses, to be polite. Then end the encounter by redirecting yourself or leaving. Be sure not to ask questions back, which will prolong the encounter because it indicates reciprocated interest.

Pursuer: So do you live around here?
You: Oh, just in the next town.
Him: And where do you work?
You: In town.
Him: What do you do?
You: Nursing. I have to be off to the hospital. Nice chatting with you.

3. *The grunt*. Make a bore of yourself by returning just monosyllabic replies or noises.

Pursuer: So do you live around here?
You: (unintelligible grunt)
Her: Well, do you work around here?
You: (unintelligible grunt)
Her: Well, see you! (Usually comes after two attempts to talk to you.)

4. *The make-like-a-banana-and-split sendoff.* If he doesn't lay off in spite of your hints, brief replies, or grunts and you feel infringed upon, try tougher tactics. Be assertive and clear.

- Adult lines:

"I'd like to concentrate on my book, so I really can't talk any more."

"I need to be alone to think about something for a while."

"Sorry, but I'm not in the mood to talk right now."

- Less grown-up lines:

"Make like a tree and leave."

"Make like a board and walk."

"Make like Goldilocks and get lost."

Sometimes I don't understand jokes told by the opposite sex.

With a sense of humor, everything from a marriage to an immune system lasts. So tickling someone's funny bone tends to bond the two of you more closely. But when a "What?" takes the place of a "Ha-ha-ha," you've flubbed a chance to connect and instead feel farther apart.

Psychologists who count laughs have discovered that men and women differ in when and why they joke. Guys more often like getting guffaws from a group and appear better than women at remembering one-liners and made-up jokes. It's not that women's brain cells don't retain punchlines, but that they just aren't as motivated to develop a storehouse of tales to get a roomful of people laughing later. In place of chuckling about the three fellows meeting St. Peter, many women prefer rehashing life's absurdities and lunatic moments. Interestingly, whether it's a sign of confidence or insecurity, women use and enjoy far more self-deprecating humor. For example, when I write on flip charts during presentations I often say, "As you can see, I didn't win the handwriting award in second grade." One study showed that 63 percent of female comics put themselves down in their act but only 12 percent of the male comics did.

Your use of humor also reflects your standing on the status ladder. Humor travels downward—once a higher-status person gets the gang going, others follow suit. A classic study of humor among hospital personnel found that the more senior a staff member was, the more he or she tended to include wit in speaking. The same study traced 99 out of 102 moments of comic relief at hospital staff meetings to men.

If his rulebook of belching doesn't break you up, if her story about spilling coffee on the CEO makes you cringe, not crack up, you're not dull, you're just stuck in The Huh? Zone, where men and women just can't get it.

Dealing with jocular differences

1. *Laugh it off*. Appreciate that life experiences fuel your sense of hilariousness. Rather than tuning out or putting down a military or mascara joke, appreciate its source. For example, men, treated to roughhousing from an early age, seem to like physical humor along the lines of The Three Stooges more than women. Feel free to express your comedic curiosity if it's killing you.

"Mikki, what is so funny about having your zipper break at a Beatles concert in 1964?"

But if you can't laugh with them, don't laugh at them.

2. *Clown around*. You'll keep the atmosphere light if you just go along with the laughers. If the men are groaning at a punchline or the ladies are hooting at the expression, "A woman without a man is like a fish without a bicycle," muster up a mirthful expression. Tip: Most women are good at pretending a Star Search reject is the life of the party, but many men need work in maintaining attention while women try out telling a joke. Remember, this may be virgin territory for her.

3. *Develop your act in mixed company*. Become more flexible in your joking style and you and others might get a greater kick from your humor. See which tactic you can use to let more laughter loose.

• Promise yourself you'll commit the best jokes you hear to memory and tell them some time in the next week. Don't worry about perfect timing. It can take a comedian a week to perfect the delivery of a story. Check bookstores for joke collections that get you slapping your knee. Good starters:

"There was something funny on the news the other day . . ."

"I heard this great story about . . ."

- Tell a story about yourself rather than a canned joke.

"This really wild thing happened yesterday at the movies . . ."

People assume I'm heterosexual, and I'm not.

Ken, a reserved fortyish pharmacist active in his college alumni group, dreaded class reunions. As a gay man, he felt uncomfortable with remarks his old friends made, like, "Aren't you going to get married one of these years?" or "Next year, bring your girlfriend along." Although Ken thought they would still accept him once they knew, he didn't feel right startling his old buddies with something blunt like, "Don't you guys know I'm gay?"

Ken was right to recognize the innocence of his classmates' assumptions, annoying as they were. In a random group, nine out of ten men *would* be heterosexual, since surveys show the incidence of homosexuality at 10 percent. Unfortunately, such assumptions create discomfort and embarrassment for those in the minority. Committed as he was to working on alumni projects, Ken knew he had to come up with a response to set these straight guys straight the next time they referred to his "wife" or "girlfriend." Here are some ideas we discussed:

Guide to coming out with it

1. *The let-them-guess approach*. Answer the question truthfully but provide no additional information. This approach fits situations where it's not the proper time, place, or context for a sexual-orientation discussion.

"No, I'm never going to get married."

"I won't be bringing a girlfriend next year."

Most folks will utter an "oh," but be ready for a "why not" or "how come?" response.

2. *The let-them-figure-it-out approach.* Strategically drop pronouns or names that recognizably belong to the unexpected sex during ordinary conversation.

"When I go out to the movies with someone, I can't stand it when he wants to analyze it afterwards."

"Miguel, the man I live with, is from Argentina and is really into polo."

3. *The let-them-be-educated approach.* If you'd like to correct the incorrect assumption, seize the moment.

"It's interesting that you assume I date women. Actually I'm not into women."

"I guess you're used to men being married or living with a woman, but if I bring a partner or lover to the reunion next year it will be a man."

4. *The break-it-to-them-gently approach.* Use these softeners to lessen the chances of flustering your listeners.

"I guess it's not obvious, and I know you may be surprised, but I haven't gotten married because I've always known I was gay."

"I hope this isn't too shocking, but I won't ever be bringing a woman to reunions because I'm gay."

5. *The I-am-who-I am approach.* This wouldn't fit Ken's personality, but it's an option when you feel right about being direct and proud.

"I'll never have a wife. I'm gay."

"I'll probably bring Miguel, my lover, next year."

Remember that you always have the right not to come out with it. Heterosexuals don't go around announcing their sexual preferences and you don't have to, either.

What's a smooth way to fix two people up?

If you have a gut feeling that two folks you know might hit it off, go for it, once you know that each is eager to meet a significant other. As the fixer upper, you may worry about coming off as a busybody. But no matter how desperately they despise each other at first sight, they'll usually appreciate your good intentions (unless, of course, you knowingly set up Cousin Sue with a serial killer). As long as you can accept that your fantastic fixup might crumble at the first hello, the odds are good that you'll someday instigate some friend's lifetime partnership. Even today in the United States, 32 percent of married couples say they met through friends or relatives, far more than through school, organizations, or work. You'll connect people with confidence if you avoid the following—

Fix-up fiascoes

- giving a friend someone's name without asking the someone first
- assuming that Ned, whom you find obnoxious, will charm the socks off your sister
- telling fixees they were made for each other before they've so much as breathed in each other's presence (too much pressure to get along!)
- fixing up two very, very quiet people (chances are, they'll each call the other boring.)
- pairing a person ready for a relationship with someone just beginning to heal from a breakup, or who insists he never wants to be trapped

- matching a duo with dueling points of view (Grant, a veterinarian, won't likely talk the night away with Leah, who hates anything four-legged.)

Instead, fix up with finesse

1. *Check availability*. Make sure each prospective fixee is available and willing to meet someone before you make your match.

2. *Promote the match*. Describe to each friend what you like or the friend might like in your potential Romeo or Juliet. Mention how you know this stranger, and portray looks, brains, and personality realistically.

"Gene's tall with a sort of rumpled look. He graduated from Dartmouth and works as a copywriter for an ad agency. He seems natural and loyal—he still hangs out with his pals from high school. I got to know him at the Arts Center photography course I took last winter."

3. *Connect them*. Give them both each other's phone number, unless one specifically requests to be the caller or the called. True, men still more often make the first move, but let them sort that out.

4. *Wait discreetly for news*. Don't call the instant after the date to learn the scoop about the setup. If a casual "How did it go?" gets only a vague "He was nice, but . . . ," don't pry. She may not want to delve into the thirty-seven ways he was a drip. If the date went well, celebrate. If not, try again. Considering the unpredictability of personal chemistry, your next match may catch fire beautifully.

Certain people touch me too much when they talk.

Research tells us that in many situations, touch can add to trust in a relationship and create positive feelings. A study in a library revealed that patrons who received a gentle pat when checking out their books held a more positive attitude toward the library than those who checked out without that human touch. But if you've had one too many pats on the back, you may be touchy about physical contact in general or sensing the other signals that can be carried in a touch.

Tactile sensitivity often arises when the touch is not reciprocal or in relationships where there's a difference in power. Not only can a supervisor initiate touch with an employee, a teacher with a student, a doctor with a patient—but not vice versa, women are touched more than men are, both by men and other women. Men touch women about twice as much as women touch men, perhaps because women know that a man may misperceive a display of warmth as a sexual come-on. Whatever the reason for your discomfort, you have the right to determine when touch is too much.

Get a grip on the situation

Figure out which of these factors explains the touch:

1. *The patter pats everyone indiscriminately.* You're not being singled out, you just happen to be more sensitive. Cultural factors may be at work here. One researcher who observed conversational pairs in coffee shops around the world counted 180 touches an hour in San Juan, 110 in Paris, none in London, and two in Gaines-

ville, Florida. Even among members of the same family, personality differences may cause half the siblings to enjoy hugs with strangers and the others to prefer to save touch for their intimate circle of friends, family, and lovers.

2. *She touches you because she likes you.* The closer you feel to someone, the more probable it is you will touch while talking. The toucher intends to demonstrate good feelings toward you. It's her way, but obviously not yours.

3. *His touching lets you know he has the upper hand.* In this situation, he probably occupies a higher status or is competitive with you. You may get particularly annoyed when the touch—

- serves no bonding purpose but feels like you're trapped or in his clutches.
- could never be appropriately initiated or even reciprocated by you.
- comes out of condescension.

(If you feel like he's your junior high school principal about to give you a detention despite the shoulder embrace, trust your instinct, not the apparent friendliness.)

Apply a hands-off solution

For situations one and two, recognize that there's a difference in style, not a deep problem. For situation three, decide how willing you are to upset the toucher by blocking his moves. Try these maneuvers when you feel that touching is getting out of hand.

1. *Keep out of arm's way.* She's less likely to touch if she has to reach farther than arm's length. You might need to stand up to five feet away from someone with long limbs.

2. *React*—as opposed to being careful not to offend. Try a quick jump, a sudden move away, body tensing, or a grimace next time. Touchers in all categories pay attention to negative feedback, since touching is a source of pleasure for them. If you're concerned about hurting category one and two's feelings, remember that you're providing an important life lesson for them: Not everyone enjoys being touched as much as they happen to enjoy touching.

3. *Tell him to lay off.* A direct reproach may feel out of the blue to the toucher, since nonverbal habits frequently exist outside of conscious awareness. Even category three doesn't usually realize his transgressions. Put your message in the form of a polite request.

"Pat, I get nervous when someone grabs my arm. Could you try not to?"

"Anita, I appreciate your enthusiasm. Can we leave out the back patting next time?"

"Ira, I feel funny saying this, but your shoulder slapping hurts."

He's too blunt/She never gets to the point.

Even when discussing a pleasant topic like where to go on vacation, Maureen and Buddy get on each others' nerves. Maureen enjoys considering all the possibilities in the travel section of the paper, daydreaming aloud about an African safari or a trip to Asia. Buddy gets exasperated that she's wasting time talking about trips they could never afford, and announces that they should go to the ranch in New Mexico that they always visit. Maureen calls Buddy a party pooper and wonders how she'll stand a week away (and a lifetime) with such an unimaginative conversationalist. For his part, Buddy complains that Maureen stretches his patience to the limit.

The male propensity to get to the point comes out of a solution-oriented, speak-up-when-you-know-exactly-what-you-mean approach to conversation. Men may consider possibilities in their heads and then present the final analysis or idea. Women, who value the process of give and take about alternatives, can be turned off by definitiveness on a problem that they feel calls for discussion. For them, meandering and digressions in conversation can feel just as satisfying as arriving at an answer.

Since time wasted to Buddy is time well spent to Maureen, they and others need a map to understand the alternative routes men and women often take to a conversational destination.

The shortcut

In this no-frills, direct style of talking, conclusions, generalizations, and the bottom line come up front. This occurs most frequently in fast-paced, task-oriented environments and is more characteristic of men than women.

Perils of the shortcut

- may appear brusque to folks who prefer a more leisurely route
- may invite unwanted argument or hostility, particularly from a nonuser
- may mistakenly (or accurately) give the impression that the speaker's mind is closed

Example: Because of the firmness of his tone and language, Maureen assumed that Buddy was determined to take her to the New Mexico ranch again. Buddy said, "I was waiting for Maureen to come up with other reasonable suggestions for a vacation, but she abruptly left the room when I mentioned New Mexico."

Mapping out some new routes

1. Include at least two points before you offer a conclusion.
   "Since we like the mountains and can always count on the great food, how about that ranch in New Mexico again?"

2. Add "What do you think?" after stating a firm idea or conclusion.

3. Use words that imply that you're not totally committed to your idea.

DON'T SAY: "We should go to the ranch again."
TRY: "I think the ranch might be a good idea."

The long and winding road

This style of talking emphasizes the fun of the journey—the conversational back and forth—with conclusions embedded in less significant points, after many points, or not included at all. It occurs most frequently when time is available, and when rapport matters more than getting a job done. In personal relationships, more women than men use this style.

Perils of the long and winding road

- may lose the listener's interest, attention, or comprehension
- may give the impression to a shortcutter that the speaker isn't logical or efficient
- may be vulnerable to interruption and losing the point that would eventually come

Example: Maureen was just about to get to the "Ranch Vacations" section of the paper when Buddy broke in.

Mapping out some new routes

1. Make no more than three points before coming to a conclusion.

155

2. Don't keep talking for more than thirty-five to forty-five seconds at a time. Study sound bites on TV and radio news to note how much key information can be conveyed in a short period of time.

3. Come right out with your point, but soften it so you won't feel like you're coming on too strong. "Well, after looking everything over, I think the Grand Canyon is our best bet."

Women tell me I'm crude.

Boorishness lies in the eye of the beholder—heck, the Romans may have loved your act. Yet if you're interested in gaining attention for your competence, not your crudeness, assess yourself and figure out what makes you uncouth. Although refined behavior is not a women-only province, certainly many members of the traditionally gentler sex mind their manners more. Besides the columnist in *Playboy*, has there been a male etiquette adviser lately? Communication researchers note subtle signs that women win in the politeness arena. They make more indirect requests, emphasize cooperation, take up less physical space, curse less, use more correct grammar and pronunciation, and smoke far fewer cigars. More women prefer ballet to boxing.

Males who rein in rough language and behavior when "fragile females" are around present a dilemma for women who wish to be treated equally. When I hear "Excuse my language" or "There are ladies present," I'm confident my credibility isn't helped by this china-doll treatment. But a whack on the shoulder and public belching don't do much for me, either. If you're getting feedback that you could use more grace and tact, take a long look at what you're doing. It could be that you're offending guys too, but they'd feel unmanly letting you know.

Getting in gear with crude control

1. *Get in neutral*. Calm down. Take an inventory of your irritating habits by observing yourself or having others give you feedback. Sam, a client who was told that his overbearing style turned off sales prospects, had colleagues fill out a crudeness evaluation form after a pre-

sentation. He learned that he had talked too loudly, made a face at someone who questioned him and scratched himself in a way that made others uncomfortable. Remember that it's not always fun to face and then lose the traits that make you obnoxious.

2. *Observe the other guys' reactions*. Focus on the impact you have on others. Notice facial expressions of distaste, physical distancing, and topic shifts which indicate that you're hard to take. Consider whether you have an ulterior motive for acting crude. According to a researcher at Virginia Tech, men may use profanity as a way to dominate in social interactions.

3. *Choose a destination*. Develop role models of finesse and graciousness you can relate to. Ask yourself if Peter Jennings would ever tell the joke about the constipated gorilla.
Pick one behavior at a time you want to eliminate.
- talking about my hernia at lunch with Martha
- chewing on an unlit cigar at sales meetings
- using the F-word every other sentence

4. *Drive ahead, and pay the tolls*. Try giving yourself a minor punishment after you've committed an uncivilized act. Inconvenience yourself enough to increase your motivation to catch yourself before you offend. For example, Sam treated his colleagues to lunch after they rated him as "grating" at a meeting.

CRUDE BUT TRUE: Men like dirty jokes better than women do. The more curse words accompanying a cartoon, the funnier the men find it.

I'm critical of someone an opposite-sex friend is involved with.

Fiona felt that putting up with Brad's late-night visits and mysterious weekend absences was worth it, considering how much Brad seemed to love her. Her pal Harvey didn't see it that way. He said that either Brad was fooling around or, worse, hiding the fact that he was married. Harvey insisted that as a male he understood Brad's modus operandi better than Fiona ever would. Fiona told Harvey that he was distrustful and overprotective of her and warned him that if he continued cutting Brad down, she would consider Harvey less of a friend.

Like Harvey, you may feel particularly entitled to an opinion about your friend's romantic problems, since you have a privileged perspective on the treatment she's receiving. A man may more easily recognize another man's commitment-phobic behavior, and a woman may rightly hear "get lost" in another woman's "Sorry, I'm busy this month." Naturally, you're also sure you're more objective. If your friend solicits your opinion about his latest romance, fine. Couch it as a guess, not the truth from on high. But beware of using your opposite-sex advantage to act as an unsolicited authority on his love life. By playing an uninvited Ann Landers, you may end up in your friend's minus column.

Advice on advice to friends

1. *Boyfriends, lend 'em your ears*. Your woman friend may be expecting you to listen, not lecture. Recognize that she may need empathy, not analysis and recommendations. Fiona felt fine for now in her unclear entanglement with Brad. Harvey was assuming that Fiona

wanted more from Brad, like marriage, and he was concerned that she not get hurt. But more than Harvey's protection, Fiona wanted a trusted friend to confide in. Harvey could have helped her more with talk that showed he understood how she felt, like "Boy, it must be hard when you're missing him and he's nowhere to be found."

2. *Girlfriends, don't get out the violin.* Male friends may feel safe sharing hurts and heartbreaks with you because you won't judge them as weak or wimpy for having strong feelings. But be careful about overdoing the sympathy ("Oh Harv, I can't believe anyone would treat a wonderful guy like you so rotten"). He may take it as condescending or overly motherly. Since he probably values solutions to his woes, ask, "Do you want my opinion on this?" or "Do you want to hear what I think is going on?"

3. *All friends, be tactful in your offerings to friends.* As an opposite-sex confidant, you may well be asked what you think of your friend's lover. If you truly sense that further involvement could spell emotional or physical harm, as a friend you need to say so. But often, your friend's attraction isn't fatal so much as hard for you to fathom. Even though Harvey thinks that Brad's a jerk, it still could work for Fiona. So try to advise without alienating with these diplomatic phrases:
   • Good points but . . .
   "He's got plenty of good points, but I'm concerned about his history of drinking."
   • Wait and see:
   "So far it's been great, but wait and see if she can really shake off her hangups from her last husband."
   • I understand your attraction, but . . .
   "I understand your attraction, but I don't really trust him yet."

"She really is sexy, but I'm not sure you get along intellectually."

• Patterns:

"You've been involved with Peter-Pan types before. Remember Bernie?"

"She reminds me of your first wife—the jealousy especially."

• Are you sure?

"Are you sure he's telling the truth about his weekend business trips?"

"I know she's acting like 'this is it,' but are you sure?"

• Personally, I think you need . . .

"Personally, I don't see him with you, Fiona. I think you need someone more available."

"Personally, I think you need someone more self-confident."

• As your friend . . .

"As your friend, I have to tell you I think Brad's being dishonest about his business trips."

"I'm saying this as a friend. She seems awfully concerned with your money."

What do you do if you're with a couple who's fighting?

Bonnie and Larry looked forward to a fun evening playing a trivia game with Todd and Edna. The gathering turned grim when Todd failed to name the only rock-and-roll singer appearing on a stamp and Edna accused him of living in a cultural vacuum. After tossing his playing piece, Todd stormed away from the table and turned on the TV loudly. While Edna went to hurl more accusations at Todd, Bonnie and Larry whispered about what to do.

Some couples feel safer airing anger in public where they won't be able to hash out genuine serious differences. For example, Edna used the "trivia test" to confront Todd with her disappointment in his lack of worldly sophistication. A few are reaching out for help and you're the hotline. Still other duos are just continuing their private dueling in public, unaffected by the usual social inhibitions. As uncomfortable as you may feel, you want to avoid making things worse by stepping into a ring where you don't know the beasts lurking behind the curtain.

When a double date turns into a circus—

1. *Stay out of the ring.* By joining one side or the other, you'll make the conflict worse. Wisely, Bonnie bit back her incredulity that Todd had missed such an easy question, while Larry resisted criticizing Edna for picking on Todd. Taking sides could damage your friendship, since a couple often agree to forgive things said by each other but not so easily what someone outside their intimate circle tosses in.

2. *Call lightly for a truce*. If you're comfortable enough with the couple and you can get a few words in edgewise, invite them to give peace a chance. Humor will help here.

"We'd love it if you'd both come back to the trivia board. I don't want to miss my chance to win for a change."

"If we sit between you at the table, can we continue the game?"

"Rule number twenty-three says you're not allowed to leave the table until someone wins. Come on, let's finish the game."

3. *File out of the grandstand*. If the duelers keep tangling and you feel uncomfortable, stand up and announce calmly that you're going home. This may have the effect of cooling them down, when the warring couple realizes the rudeness of ruining your evening too. If the onlookers to the tiff are also the hosts, bringing the duelers back to their role as guests with humor could be helpful.

"Hope you two don't start throwing our good china. Should we leave?"

4. *Check the reviews afterwards*. When good friends of yours appear to be at each other's throats, or can't get through dinner without losing their cool, you can show you care by calling and opening the door for them to talk about what's wrong.

"Todd, you and Edna really seemed teed off the other night. Is everything OK?"

"Edna, did you and Todd work things out after we left?"

My partner's family asks questions I consider very personal.

No matter how entitled someone feels to answers about your personal affairs, you don't have to oblige if a question reaches into territory that you want to keep private. Although you may be tempted to respond, "That's none of your business," tact is necessary when you hope to avert a family feud. Be aware that relatives may view you as an inside track for the lowdown they'd be uncomfortable requesting directly from your mate. Try these wiles to guard your secrets with a smile.

Holding back answers without giving offense

1. *Change the subject.* Deflect the question by making a segue onto a related but innocuous conversational track.

Questioner: "Gil, is Gina off her diet again?"

You: "I'm not sure if dieting really works. I read a new study that says that the most effective weight-loss method is walking half an hour a day."

2. *Generalize.* Instead of answering the specific question, give a broad answer that doesn't reveal anything personal.

Questioner: "Why does Bobby [your son] keep switching schools? Is he having academic problems?"

You: "Lots of kids have a hard time finding themselves in this day and age."

3. *Exaggerate.*

Questioner: "It's great that you finally found a job. How much will they be paying you?"

You: "Gee, I think he said close to a million."

4. *Use humor*.

Questioner: "So when are you going to drop those excess pounds?"

You: "I don't know. I'm trying to stay eligible for the Roseanne Arnold and Oprah Winfrey Commiseration Club."

5. *Apologize with the "I promised not to tell" excuse*. Blame your inability to tell on a policy of someone else.

Questioner: "How much did you pay for your car?"

You: "It was such a deal that I promised the salesman I wouldn't jeopardize his job by telling."

6. *Play dumb*. Master the utterance "I don't know."

Questioner: "How are your stocks doing?"

You: "I haven't really checked on them lately."

7. *Share another secret*. Reward your interrogator's curiosity with personal information you don't mind sharing that she might find just as valuable.

Questioner: "When are you two going to have children?"

You: "Listen, don't go around telling people, but we've put in an application to the Peace Corps."

His relatives won't refer to me by the last name I use.

Barbara Kane had more pragmatic than political reasons for keeping her name when she married. She'd owned a successful mall boutique, Kane's Korner, for ten years and enjoyed being identified as its owner. But her in-laws, the Snows, addressed all correspondence to her and their son as "Mr. and Mrs. John Snow." When Papa Snow introduced her to distant relatives at a family party as "Barbie Snow," Barbara chided, "My name is Kane, not Snow." Her father-in-law responded, "You married my son and he's a Snow," and Barbara was ready to divorce her in-laws on the spot.

When your in-laws call you by the wrong name, they're engaging in some wish fulfillment. They believe that in order to be a real family, you must share everything, including a last name. Though you and your spouse may be perfectly comfortable with different last names, Mom and Dad may worry that unusual name choices bode ill for your union. Recall that you too are making a statement by keeping your name—you show that you want to preserve an independent identity. Mates who hyphenate, as in John and Cara Wiley-Fitch, demonstrate that they value equality.

Since our name is one of the basics about us, we expect people who care to get it right, even though they don't share our views. Here are some ways to help the relatives attach the right name to your face.

Getting others in step with your name

1. *Spell it out*. Don't assume relatives will absorb your choice of names from one or two return addresses.

When you marry, divorce, or change your name for the heck of it, be explicit about who the new or old you is.

"John and I will hyphenate our last names, so it will be John and Cara Wiley-Fitch."

"I didn't change my name when we got married, so it's still Barbara Kane, just like before."

2. *Spell it out again.* At the first misnaming, gently correct. Assume that Mom and Pop are not purposely offending.

"Oh, you forgot. It's Wiley-Fitch, not Wiley."

"Remember, my name is still Barbara Kane."

"From now on, could you write 'Dr. and Dr.' on the envelope? Both Lila and I are M.D.'s."

3. *Keep it out in front.* Forestall forgetting with these more aggressive tactics:

• At social gatherings with the family, introduce yourself first.

• Have your mate purposely refer to you by the correct name in front of the offenders.

"The other day my dentist asked me, 'Are you Barbara Kane's husband?' "

4. *Drop it.* If three or four tries at correction fail, don't let the name issue drive you insane. Relatives' prejudices, mental blocks, or insensitivities are unfortunate but relatively painless. Keep on correcting, but do less expecting that they'll change.

PROFESSIONALLY
SPEAKING

I'm concerned that my innocent comments may be taken as harassment.

Monitoring what comes out of our mouths with the opposite sex in the workplace makes good sense. Women especially are more attuned than ever to words that ruin a workday or worse. The most damaging and offensive verbal sexual harassment accompanies job hiring or firing ("I'd love to have you on board if you'll get together with me after work") or creates an intimidating work environment (This is what Clarence Thomas was accused of having done when he allegedly persisted in pornographic talk to Anita Hill). Be aware that even when you *mean* no harm with references to your colleague's or your own looks, body, sexual acts, desires, or habits, she may feel mistreated or uncomfortable.

Caroline mentioned to her boss, Daryl, one Monday that she had done some gardening over the weekend. He smiled at her and joked, "You must look great on your knees." A month later Daryl received a letter from the firm's equal opportunity officer informing him of a complaint by Caroline of a pattern of sexual harassment. After expressing shock that Caroline had registered a formal complaint, Daryl insisted that he and Caroline had been enjoying harmless banter for months. But he had misread her signals, giving his joke a disastrous punchline. As with all matters related to sex, Daryl needed to be more careful.

Safe talk with the opposite sex: Preventing verbal sexual harassment

1. *Abstinence*. You'll never get in trouble by refraining from all sexually related talk. Don't assume that becoming friendly at work means sexual comments become appropriate. If you feel compelled to provoke or include such talk, with or without leers, pats, brushes, or other sexually suggestive behavior, you need to control yourself or seek help.

2. *Proceed with caution*. When you're bursting with the urge to share an off-color joke, tell a mild one and observe the reaction. If your listener responds with a bawdy story of her own, gives a belly laugh, or asks if you know any others, chances are that she enjoyed your offering. But watch for signs that she's turned off—these mean you'll have to muzzle yourself:

- He blushes, gives a nervous laugh, fidgets, or gives other physical signs of discomfort or confusion. You're making a harasser of yourself. Stop!
- She avoids you or ignores your comments by changing the subject. One survey reported that 76 percent of harassed women used the ignoring strategy, though the harasser frequently didn't get the message to change his behavior.
- He's silent. Caroline, like many people, showed her discomfort this way. Daryl should have noticed.
- She asks you to stop. This takes courage for many people, especially if you're higher up on the

totem pole. Someone who asks you to stop certainly means it.

3. *Recoup your mistake*. Own up if you get the slightest sign that you've offended. The harasser's insensitivity is what sends verbal victims straight to the personnel office. Your offense may be overlooked if you apologize and refrain from doing it again.

"I didn't mean to be crude. Please forgive me."

"Uh-oh, that just slipped out, and I offended you. I'm sorry."

"Now I've gone and made a jerk of myself! I'm sorry."

"Can I take that comment back? That was inappropriate."

I'm uncomfortable talking to an audience of the opposite sex.

Though the workplace has become increasingly gender integrated since the 1960s, many speaking situations with a nearly unisex audience remain. Since women comprise only 2 percent of top management in corporate America, an executive woman often finds herself the sole representative of her sex in the boardroom. As Jill, a sophisticated head of human resources in a major hotel chain, told me, "I don't like it when I'm the only executive in earrings." Though far from the frilly type, Jill wanted feedback about whether her delivery was either too sweet or too strong—reasonable concerns for women presenting to mostly male audiences.

Men speak less of feeling threatened by an all-female audience and often joke about enjoying the attention. But the Svengali approach has its pitfalls. Jack, a salesman for an educational publisher who was blessed with cover-guy looks, felt he didn't have to work too hard when he had an audience of elementary school teachers. According to Jack, the teachers were thrilled to see a halfway decent-looking man in front of them. He was shocked when his supervisor told him to tone down his sex appeal. He had thought it was his major selling point.

Advice to Jack and Jill on speaking to opposite-sex audiences

For Jill, to get to the top of the hill—

1. *Don't act girlish, sexy, or silly.* Some men might like you, but they won't respect you. Use a confident

nonverbal demeanor—feet about even with shoulders, gestures that are above the waist and outstretched. Avoid looking small by slouching, sitting in an oversized chair, or standing behind a lectern.

2. *Do be moderate in appearance and manner*. Resist anything which takes attention away from business—too much perfume, too-high heels, too-short skirts, too-striking colors, and of course, references to baking or mascara.

3. *Don't be put off by stone faces*—men tend to display less facial expression than women. Don't make an issue of chivalry, either. Twelve board members rising when you enter the room is gallant to them, not patronizing. (But see "People at work call me 'honey' and I hate it" on handling endearments. [p. 227])

4. *Do monitor communication habits that may undercut your message*. Some male audiences value logical over emotional expression. Be yourself but also:

- Be direct, not wordy.
- Show comfortable but not overly emotional facial expressions.
- Avoid asking for approval, directly or indirectly. Focus on the ideas, not your value as a presenter.

DON'T SAY: "Did I get my point across?"
TRY: "Can I add anything to further your understanding of the proposed development site?"

- Use a downward pitch at the end of sentences.

DON'T SAY: "This collection has been poorly received in the California stores?" (As if you're asking for confirmation of something you know to be true.)

TRY: "This collection has been poorly received in the California stores."

- Leave out overly dramatic expressions of emotion, such as:
"This plan is *soooo* effective."
"We're really, truly ready for a fantastic reorganization."

For Jack, to avoid falling down and breaking your crown—

1. *Don't assume you can do no wrong just because you wear pants.* Women are just as critical in judging male speakers.

2. *Do be sure to include examples and appeals to emotions in your talk, not just facts and data.* This engages all audiences, and especially those in people-oriented professions.

3. *Don't act in a way that comes off as authoritative or arrogant.* Female audiences will interpret your style as condescending. Don't—

- Give an order: "You will each need to order a sample kit."
- Attack opponents' positions: "I don't see how you could think the old textbook covers the fundamentals better than our new version."
- Be blindly judgmental: "We have no competition. They're all losers."
- Use endearments—Why? See "People at work call me 'honey' and I hate it." (p. 227)
- Call women girls.

176

4. *Do show warmth by getting involved with the audience, learning their names, engaging in small talk, and even offering a self-deprecatory remark here and there.*

"My wife tells me I sometimes go on and on when I'm trying to make a point. So don't be polite—interrupt me."

I need to hold people's attention when I speak.

You're right to be concerned about keeping your audience alert—a majority of executives in one survey admitted that they'd dozed off during at least one dry delivery the preceding year. Like other presentation coaches, I've observed that each sex has characteristic dispiriting and vitalizing patterns of speech. More women use varied intonation, hitting a greater range of notes in what specialists call vocal variety. Even expressive women can get boring to listen to, though, if each sentence contains a similar intonation pattern for a singsong effect. Since women tend to use more precise pronunciation, correct grammar, and less slang than men, they run the danger of sounding too polished and controlled.

On the other side of the fence, men may compensate for less interesting intonation by having a richer voice resonance or tone and lower vocal pitch. Additionally, men's propensity for louder volume adds to their ability to hold an audience's attention.

Donna, an ophthalmologist who presented her cornea research at international conferences, showed the strict speech training she had received as a girl by pronouncing every "ing," "ed," and "t" to the hilt. That and the constant rhythm she used in her sentences helped someone in nearly every audience of hers nod out. Even at home, her speech was so perfect that callers sometimes took her for a recording when she answered the phone. Vic, her colleague at the medical school, demonstrated male pattern boredom—minimal shifts in pitch and volume, a tired drop to the lowest note and weakest volume at the end of sentences. To cure droopy eyelids, both Donna and Vic needed to add animation to their delivery.

From soporific to spellbinding

1. *Add zip to certain words.* Give your listeners a lift by emphasizing one word in every phrase. Make this word

- higher
- louder, or
- longer

Hint: Emphasize adjectives (an *outstanding* event), numbers (*50* percent more effective), or strong verbs (he *flew* across the ballfield).

2. *Keep your energy up.* Many speakers start off with pep and then fizzle into a flat delivery. If you're speaking at length, give yourself reminders to keep feeding the enthusiasm engine. (Vic wrote "vv" on the margins of his presentation overheads to remind him to use vocal variety.)

3. *Men: Stretch your vocal reach.* Many men have trouble making their voices go higher on key words. To become more persuasive, see if you can go up a half step or a whole step on the words indicated in these phrases:

THIS can make a difference.
This CAN make a difference.
This can MAKE a difference.
This can make a DIFFERENCE.

Practice this exercise while reading a book or newspaper aloud for five minutes a day.

4. *Women: Dare to be different.* Get out of the perfect mold by speaking each sentence in a distinct, even surprising, way. Some ideas:

- Vary the length of sentences as well as pauses within or between sentences to let information sink in.

"What we need—(pause) and I'm confident we can pull this off in the third quarter—(pause) is a push toward total quality management."

- Stretch out the vowel in a word for a richer and bolder sound.

"She's got the riiiight stuff!"

- Vary your volume. If you tend to be a loud-mouth, occasionally say a sentence more quietly. You'll sound more intimate or confidential. If you're on the softspoken side, go louder on the points you want to emphasize. You'll come across as more persuasive.

I wish my voice sounded more professional.

In research conducted about the impressions given by male and female voices, women's voices were judged less authoritative and professional. There are two sides to this sound and sex story, though. A survey conducted by the Institute for Applied Psychology found that catastrophes didn't seem as dreadful when reported by a female broadcaster.

Communication researchers have also discovered differing ideal voice characteristics for men and women. One recent study asked people to describe the ideal voice in general and then the ideal male and ideal female voice. Both the general ideal and ideal male pitch were low, but the ideal female pitch was medium. Because so many prominent women broadcasters have low-pitched voices and because of the great admiration among my clients for the Lauren Bacall/Kathleen Turner image, I suspect the ideal female pitch tends toward low as well. People also preferred women to have a softer volume than what they considered ideal in general and ideal for males. So a woman who speaks on the louder side may be judged more harshly than a man at the same decibel level. Apparently men are allowed more vocal range. A throaty vocal quality—characteristic, for example, of both Kirk and Michael Douglas—was perceived as unintelligent, uninteresting, and cloddish in women but evidence of sophistication and adjustment coming out of a man's mouth.

This is not to say that men can assume their voices naturally project the influential image they want. I've coached numerous men who spoke at such a low pitch that they had little room for expressive variety. Others had a monotonous tone or needed to learn how to adjust volume and rate to those they were communicating with.

Both sexes can profit from some tips to ensure that their voices are professionally sound.

Sounds of sex-sess

1. *Sound as rich and as warm as you can.* You need to work on this if people consider you stiff, formal, or distant on account of your voice, or if your voice comes across as less than adult. By making your voice more resonant and rounded, though not louder, you'll sound like a million bucks. Picture your voice as a wide arrow beginning in your abdomen, gliding through your vocal cords, and filling up your mouth before it leaves to reach its target. Practice with one-syllable words to start. Men with deep voices that are also rich need to pay special attention to clarity, word endings, and pronunciation, which almost get lost at times in their mellifluous tones.

To sound warm, imagine that you're softly pouring out your words rather than firing them in rapid succession. Relaxing your vocal cords by yawning and then letting out a sigh once or twice a day will help. Rather than a drill sergeant barking out orders, you'll sound more like the nurse of your dreams.

2. *Sound strong, but not too strong.* Both sexes will sound more persuasive when their volume stays in the medium range. Men may want to be particularly aware of adjusting their decibel level downward in a group of women or when talking to softspoken folks of either sex. I've worked with many quiet clients, mostly women but some men, who associate increased intensity with sounding angry. These folks need feedback from a coach who will let them know that a more effective volume does not sound furious.

3. *Sound deep but not too deep.* Both men and women do best when they center pitch around the medium to lower notes in their range. People with lower voices are judged to be more relaxed, socially engaging, and believable. But if you go too low, you'll get a tired, crackly sound called a "fry." To find a comfortably deep pitch, take a relaxed, long breath and say "uh-huh" on the exhalation. This simple method helps you locate your personal best note. Keep in mind that both men and women can have physical causes for an overly high or low pitch, so seek out a speech pathologist specializing in voice for any serious concerns.

Extreme pitch changes, more likely in women because of their greater vocal expressiveness, can be jolting to listeners. One woman attorney had mastered what she called a "Jane Pauley pitch." Unfortunately, she had neglected to modify the pitch of her laughter as well, which sounded hyenalike when we recorded her end of a phone conversation.

People pay more attention to men's input at our meetings.

Many of my women clients confess that they feel least competent at work meetings. The challenge of speaking up at all, getting a word in edgewise, holding the floor and having their opinions respected makes the weekly strategy meeting seem like communication combat. They haven't suddenly regressed from superwoman to a speechless sap, I assure them. The obstacles to women communicating in mixed group situations are well documented and important for both sexes to know.

Of meetings and men

The following communication behaviors, used unconsciously by men, increase their comfort and women's discomfort:

- talking more in general
- initiating more topics, opinions, solutions
- interrupting others, especially women
- not paying attention to others' comments, particularly women's
- ignoring topics others bring up
- answering questions not addressed to them
- speaking loudly, long, and with direct language

Note: Even in grade school, with mostly female teachers, boys receive more attention, encouragement, and airtime in the classroom.

Of meetings and women

The following communication behaviors, used unconsciously by women, increase their discomfort and reinforce the behavior of men:

- not initiating topics
- yielding to a topic someone else brings up
- infrequently "calling" someone on an interruption
- falling silent if their ideas aren't noticed
- offering support and agreement more than adding ideas
- using soft voices—sometimes literally not being heard
- just watching

Meeting in the middle

These communication strategies, if used consciously by men and women, will increase women's comfort at meetings while allowing men to maintain their strength in a mixed group.

Men:

1. Your colleagues have a right not to be interrupted. Start speaking after she completes her idea.
2. Control your tendency to add your own opinion before reacting to the validity of others' ideas. Begin your contributions with inclusive and supportive reactions such as these:
"Regarding Mary Ann's idea . . ."
"There are pros and cons to an interdepartmental training session."
"What she says makes a lot of sense to me."

3. Recognize that you may have more experience than women when it comes to speaking in a group. Actively solicit a female colleague's input, especially if she is new to that particular group.

   "Tracey, what ideas do you have about cross-departmental training?"
4. Stop talking so much. Over the course of a collaborative meeting, participation that runs about equal between the sexes will be most valuable.

Women:

1. Speak up early in the meeting to get warmed up.
2. Practice jumping in on the heels of someone's comment. In a fast-paced group, waiting just an extra second means you lose your turn.
3. Take up space physically and verbally. Be seen in a group by sitting tall, putting hands outstretched on the table, and choosing a spot near the leader. Force yourself to speak a certain number of times per meeting, regardless of the reaction you get. Use a volume slightly louder than your usual one.
4. Beware of yielding too much. Remember these phrases, which allow you to continue your thought when interrupted:

   "Let me finish, Fred."

   "As I was saying . . ."

   You'll be interrupted less when you preface your remarks so the group knows where you're headed.

   "Let me outline three points for an ideal training plan."
5. Vary the type of comment you make. Besides statements indicating agreement, support, and praise, try these kinds of contributions:

- disagreement
- elaboration on another's comments
- switch of focus in a new direction
- a carefully thought-out opinion with backup
- summary of where the group has been and needs to go

He/she always interrupts me.

Both sexes can perpetrate and suffer interruptions. Yet communication researchers have repeatedly found that from the age of three on, males tend to intercept and females tend to pass the conversational ball. The right to interrupt or dominate a conversation often serves as an expression of superiority or status. Nevertheless, when women yield the floor to men, it is not so much a display of inferiority as an indication of the importance they attach to accommodating others in conversation.

Even conversationally accommodating people can come off as interlopers. Women like to overlap a speaker with words of encouragement, agreement, or a parallel situation. ("I know what you mean, Bill. My family also had to struggle to make ends meet.") Though she intends to establish empathy, she may annoy a man who doesn't value verbal displays of support. ("That wasn't my point. Let me finish.")

Men also complain that women disrupt their concentration when they need total focus on a project—or even the newspaper. Some researchers believe women have greater ability than men to focus on more than one stimulus at a time. So while she may not consider interrupting him watching the nightly news as a big deal, he may experience it as a rude disturbance.

Tina was sure her lab partner was a conversational clod. Right when she was getting to her point, Rich would speak up and steer the conversation in a totally new direction. Rich insisted that they didn't have to be overly polite with each other, and wondered why Tina didn't just butt in back. Tina didn't think that returning boorishness was a solution. She wanted to know if Rich's steamrolling was remediable. We discussed the Five I's for:

188

Interceding with an interrupter

Ignore him. You can't be interrupted against your will.
Next time you're tempted to yield, remember that you
have the right of way. Helpful ignorers:
>Put your index finger up.
>"Let me finish."
>"My turn now—hold it."
>"I was saying that . . ."
>Or, Tina's favorite, "Yo, Rich, I'm up at bat now."

Interpret the interruptions. Look at the patterns in the
interference. What's the intention of the interrupter?
What purpose does impeding you serve?
- to tune you out
  He: "We have to make sure to buy—"
  She: "My mother's visiting this Sunday."
- to be one up
  She: "We have to make sure to buy test—"
  He: "I told you that company's glass wasn't strong
  enough."
- to help you out
  He: "We have to make sure to buy test tube—"
  She: "Yeah, let's put in a big order this time."

Inform him. Let him know you've caught him in the act,
and share how you feel.
>"Just now I was talking about ordering supplies and
you started talking about your periodontal problems out
of the blue."
>"I was trying to explain how my parents never had any
money, and you started talking about your family."

Indicate a better way to interact with you.
>"I'd appreciate it if you'd let me finish my story."
>"I wish you'd wait until I finished my sentence."

"I'm talking about our test-tube order. When I'm done we can talk about your mother's visit."

"Talk to me after I finish reading the paper."

Instruct the innocent. If someone's interruption patterns are pervasive (she interrupts everyone), it could be that she never learned the rules for polite patter. Like a small child, she interrupts whenever a thought comes to mind, or because she's excited about sharing. Give her these basic instructions for the innocent offender:

1. Don't pounce. Do not jump in when he's uh-ing, umm-ing or still has his mouth in a ready-to-speak position. For advanced interruption control, wait two seconds before adding your two cents.
2. Inhibit your impulses. Don't express every thought the moment you have it. Stop and weigh whether an idea would contribute to the conversation or derail it.
3. Back off politely. Conversational etiquette requires you to say, "Go ahead" or "Sorry" if you mistakenly step on his sentence.

My physical size sometimes makes me feel out of place.

Although males on average surpass females in size, behavior contributes at least as much to situations where women feel small among men or men feel overbearing among women. In the human world, as in the animal kingdom, we attribute power and influence to those who stake out territory by spreading out and acting as if they own the place.

One study found that boys took up 1.2 to 1.6 times the amount of space that girls did during outdoor play. Another study revealed that on airplanes, men commandeered the arm rest between seats five times more than women. Curiously, whether the man was actually larger than the woman and so needed or deserved the extra space didn't make a difference. Apparently women unconsciously yield space to men, allowing them the most powerful seat at the table (Dad's chair) and more room on the sidewalk. One researcher in Atlanta noted that women pedestrians waiting at a traffic light moved to get out of the way of men who approached the corner. Add to these patterns men's longer strides while walking and their freedom to cross and uncross legs in all kinds of unladylike positions, and males certainly win as the more spaced-out sex.

Liza, a new high school teacher, felt like a schoolgirl whenever she met with her principal, Ross. Although his tone was collegial, she felt intimidated by his greater height and bulk. Since she couldn't will a growth spurt for herself or physical shrinkage for him, Liza was glad to know that physical size needn't rule their interactions. She could learn to take up more space, while Ross could learn to give it up.

191

Space wars (Using it and losing it with the opposite sex)

1. *Know what your space signals are saying*. Size up your universe and how you are moving through it. Notice your gait, your posture, how much room you and your things take up, and the expansiveness of your gestures. The more space you take up relative to him or her, the more dominant you will appear. Conversely, the more you condense relative to your communication partner, the weaker or more subordinate you will seem.

Liza observed that when she met with Ross, he often had his feet atop his desk, with his hands behind his head or waving a pencil in the air. Meanwhile she sat motionless in an oversized chair, looking as small as she felt.

2. *Know where you want to land*. Adjust your place in space depending on the image you want to create. Men and women who want an equal spatial relationship should explore some new territory:

Men:

To avoid being the Big Dipper, contain your gestures nearer to your body, don't take up more than your share of a couch, avoid sitting with legs too far apart or stretched out, and make sure your papers and stuff don't spill over onto her side of the table. As a supposedly egalitarian leader, Ross needed to rearrange his office demeanor to appear less dominant with his female teachers.

Women:

Expand your horizons if you're tired of being the Little Dipper. Take the dominant seat at the head of a table, choose a seat that is neither lilliputian nor gargantuan. Use longer strides and more vigorous arm movements when walking. Make gestures that reach above and beyond the breadth of your shoulders, avoid tucking in your legs while seated so they almost disappear, and watch out for folding your hands like an angel. Liza found that letting loose her natural gestures and asking to meet Ross in the teachers' lounge instead of the office expanded her presence and confidence at their meetings.

If you don't look overbearing or overwhelmed, congratulations. Your space mission has been accomplished.

I'd like to convey authority without coming across as a bitch.

While research shows few differences in communication style between male and female managers, a no-nonsense woman manager may be judged more harshly than a male counterpart with the same take-charge behaviors. When Roseanne became director of marketing at a large suburban mall, she emulated Roy, who had preceded her in the position. She gave directives to subordinates in a clear loud voice, avoided personal conversations, and controlled the emotions she expressed. Yet where Roy had been considered a "decent guy," Roseanne heard through the grapevine that she'd been dubbed "The General." Roseanne thought the way she was perceived was unfair, and asked me if requiring her department to attend a consciousness-raising seminar was her only defense. I told her about the—

Two Be's to forestall the b-word

1. *Be prepared.* Accept some tradeoff as a peculiarity of today's working environment for women. Since many people expect women to act nice and affirming, no matter where they sit on the totem pole, the higher your perch, the less you may be liked. Your attempts to be straightforwardly professional may be resented by some and respected by others.

Roseanne realized that she could not control coworkers' expectations, a reality she described aptly as "a real bitch!" But the second "Be" gave her some measure of control.

194

2. *Be strategic.* Be aware that extreme deviations from gender expectations tend to bring on the most punitive perceptions. People expect women to add "please" or softening phrases like "if you don't mind" to requests, while they expect men to skip the polite tags and be more direct, as in "Get me the Safety Committee file."

You're too weak and meek if as the boss you—

- avoid decisions
- have to have consensus
- focus on your staff's happiness rather than getting the job done
- usually yield to others' opinions
- forgive job failures easily
- frequently seek out superiors' approval
- look, speak, and act soft and frilly

You're too rough and tough if as the boss you—

- give orders and command
- threaten or punish
- rarely involve supervisees in decision making
- have a closed-door policy
- neglect expressions of emotional support
- focus single-mindedly on getting the job done
- look, speak, and act rude or severe

You're just right if as the boss you—

- React flexibly, with a focus on relationship building or job performance as the situation demands.

Roseanne recalled having denied her art director

Jay time off to see his daughter in a school play. She'd insisted that he stay at work to finish the artwork for promoting Good Health Week at the mall in plenty of time for their temperamental printer to have the lee-way he'd needed in the past. Now she realized that what Jay had argued at the time was true—he'd never missed a deadline in his life—and that she'd missed a chance to display goodwill.

• Communicate how you work and how you expect others to work. Let your staff know up front how decisions will be made and what their roles will be. Examples:

"I'll get your input at Friday's meeting and then decide."

"I'll be spelling out the new sick-leave policy in a memo."

• Empower your subordinates by listening to their ideas, encouraging innovation, developing their career paths, and providing specific positive and con-structive feedback. Remember that the more power they feel, the less likely they are to resent yours.

After our meeting, Roseanne decided to interview each staff member about his or her ideas for enhancing the mall marketing effort. This began to cut down on the number of hostile remarks they made behind her back.

Can I show concern without being considered a wimp?

Perhaps you feel like my client Jim who said he didn't know if he was supposed to supervise like Alan Alda or Attila the Hun. Studies show that both men and women managers view the bottom line as their top priority, but that women more often tune in to others' troubles, offering advice, and showing concern for employees' welfare. Depending on the macho factor in a particular company, a male supervisor may court being seen as soft when he is appropriately sensitive to a subordinate's needs.

Jorge, a new director of operations for a prestigious manufacturing firm, prided himself on his compassion for the fifty-two folks in his department. When his assistant Lance found himself in the midst of a traumatic divorce, Jorge spent several hours a week coaching him with what he'd learned from his own breakup two years before. Then one Monday he arrived at work to find a sign on his office door that read, "Ann Landers/Come right in." Jorge felt hurt and worried that his door—and his heart—were too wide open. He needed to learn—

How to be sensitive and still sensible

1. *Reassure yourself.* Responding to actual needs doesn't make you a wimp. A wimp sacrifices his sense of purpose and pride to every whim of an employee. A wimp can't tell the difference between an employee who genuinely needs help and one who asks for constant handouts. If colleagues give you flak for being a soft supervisor, don't wimp out. Stick up for your sensitive and sensible style. Sample defenses:

"I find listening helps my guys be more productive."

"It's not right to ignore someone who's obviously in trouble."

"What affects my folks affects this whole company."

2. *Listen, but within limits.* Hear her problems, express your concern, and then be explicit about how helpful you can be. Limit-setting lines:

"I'd like to hear more, but we both have to get back to the plant."

"This stuff sounds pretty painful. I hope you have some people to talk to outside of work."

Note: If her problems are interfering with work, you have the right to say so and suggest she seek assistance.

"Obviously this is a hard time for you and it's a strain for you to take calls. Would you consider talking to one of the employee assistance counselors?"

3. *Watch out for getting hooked.* Careful, Jorge. At times, helping an employee with his problems indirectly serves to help you in your own healing. Outside of work, you and Lance can talk divorce till dawn. But at the workplace, other employees will notice and wonder if the only route to equal footing is to develop marital crises of their own. You're too concerned about an employee if—

- you become as distracted by her problems as she is.
- you're the main person she talks to.
- you brood about her concerns after work.
- you're more concerned about her problems than her work.

When Jorge suggested a support group for Lance to join and kept his own advice to one coffee break a week, he was back on track as a committed and caring manager.

As a leader of a meeting, should I expect women and men to make decisions differently?

Dave, the international marketing manager for a large computer firm, confided that he enjoyed running meetings comprised mainly of women. Dave felt that women tended to make decisions without making his blood pressure rise, but that men always had a hidden agenda— outdoing the rest of the guys in the room. To a certain extent, Dave has it right. One researcher set up mock jury deliberations and studied the difference between male and female communication behaviors. Men expressed disagreement or antagonism twice as often as women, and spent more time in verbal problem solving. In comparison, women more frequently showed positive reactions to others such as agreement and understanding. Other researchers concluded that the only significant gender difference in leadership style is that men tend to be more top-down and directive in decision making than women.

Women in meetings with men need to understand that competition and struggle can be a way of reaching an amicable decision. Men in meetings with women need to see the benefits of collaborative decision making, and not to assume that unexpressed conflicts don't exist.

Whether you favor consensus or contention to settle questions, you'll be better prepared with these tips on—

Men, women, and decisions

For men in meetings with mostly women:

Expect less
- open disagreement
- interruptions
- talking time per person
- pressuring and strong language
- proving others wrong

Expect more
- focus on consensus building and fairness
- support for others' opinions
- use of team language ("We" versus "I")
- probing and elaboration of others' points of view
- nonverbal signs of interest

For women in meetings with mostly men:

Expect less
- overt support of others' ideas
- nonverbal display of interest
- focus on coming to agreement
- attentive listening
- concern about conflict

Expect more
- direct argumentation
- emphasis on winning
- interruptions of others
- focus on the most logical solution
- friendliness between "combatants"

When someone cries at work,
I can't handle it.

In a survey of working adults by psychologists at Vanderbilt University, 50 percent of men and 80 percent of women admitted having cried on the job at one time or another. The researchers also found that the tears were less damaging than the tendency of others discomfited by the crying to halt the business at hand and remain stalled.

Though crying at work seems extreme and unprofessional, it stems from an elemental human response to grief, frustration, and anger. (Is there any one of us who didn't waaaaa in the nursery some time ago?) As children, girls are coddled more when they cry, while boys receive the message once they hit kindergarten that tears mean they're a wimp. In the grown-up world, the range of situations where we tolerate male tears is extremely limited. It was OK for George Bush to wipe an eye while delivering a eulogy for the soldiers entombed in the U.S.S. *Arizona* in Pearl Harbor, but not on an equally solemn occasion, his announcement of war with Iraq. Tears from women in business or public situations may be less surprising, but they still often make the others around wonder what they should do.

Because of all our cultural conditioning, men tend to be more at a loss when a co-worker cries. With a few reminders about crying, you should be able to deal appropriately with weeping colleagues.

How to handle crying without dying

1. *Put the crying in perspective*. Tears don't signal that your colleague is on the verge of collapse. They can mean that he feels angry, sad, happy, or frustrated—or

that she has a piece of dust in her eye. Something is bothering the crier, that's all that you know.

2. *Show concern in a way both of you can take.* Any of the following will work:

- Acknowledge the crying simply, as with "Something is bothering you."
- Ask what's up, but don't push.
- Ask if you can be helpful.
- Ask if he'd like some time alone.

3. *Talk to chronic criers when they're not upset.* If you're the boss, you're entitled to bring up crying as a problem if it affects productivity or morale.

"When you cry every time I give you feedback about reports, it's difficult to feel we're making headway with their accuracy. Is there some way I can approach this so that it's less upsetting?"

I cry easily and it hurts me professionally.

Though crying has little bearing on competence, the business world associates weepiness with weakness. If you cry on the job, you probably won't be tapped for crisis management or promotion to a more demanding position. Candace, editorial manager of a daily county newspaper, stayed cool in the newsroom despite the enormous stress of deadlines and unexpected crises. I met her after a prestigious regional paper approached her to develop a new section. Candace wanted the job but dreaded the interview. Though she coped well with grilling others, when someone was firing questions at her, she sometimes found it hard to hold back tears. Candace welcomed my three-pronged program for remaining dry-eyed or in control of the situation even if the tears began to fall.

Know why you cry

Learn to identify your triggers. Do you cry when you're—

- put on the spot?
- being criticized or judged?
- giving criticism?
- angry?
- hearing or remembering something sad?
- tired?
- frustrated?
- relieved or happy?
- nervous or afraid?
- overwhelmed?
- premenstrual?

If crying stems from an unhealthy work situation, a life crisis, or chronic stress, seek professional help.

Control tears before they roll

Whenever you face one of your tear-jerker situations, prepare yourself with one of these prevention strategies:

1. *Distraction*. Squeeze your thumb and middle finger together, grip hard on your pen, or tense your toes to let stress out in less public ways.

2. *Self-talk*. Tell yourself internally that you can handle the situation effectively without crying and that even if you do weep it's not the end of the world.

3. *Visualization*. Prior to an iffy circumstance, close your eyes and picture yourself looking and sounding comfortable. Or picture yourself wet-eyed but still coming across well.

4. *Pacing*. Speak a bit more slowly and deliberately in stressful situations. Allow yourself to breathe more deeply than usual, and you'll maintain composure.

If you cry, you won't die

When prevention fails and you begin to shed tears, you can still emerge strong.

1. *If it's just a minor misty eye, don't mention it*. Your listener might assume your contact lenses or allergies are acting up.

2. *If tears become very obvious, reassure your listeners before they freak out.* Then continue to talk even though you're crying.

"I know you're not used to people getting teary at your questions. I'm fine, though. Let me tell you about how our paper covers the many ethnic groups in our county."

3. *If you feel like you're about to sob, politely excuse yourself from the situation if you can.* Duck into the rest room and let it all out. Sure, they'll wonder if it was something they did or said. Let them. When you return, apologize for the disruption, then carry on.

> Tearful truth: The average American man cries once a month, the average American woman four times a month.

My colleague can't bear any conflict.

Guy and Walt, partners in a management consulting firm, frequently clashed about expense priorities. Walt wanted to buy more sophisticated computer equipment to keep an edge over the competition, but Guy, conservative by nature, thought Walt's proposals were wasteful. After a loud shouting match over whether to purchase a color copier, Frieda, their female associate, entreated, "If you guys keep this up, I'm going to develop an ulcer. I thought we were adults."

Guy and Walt were puzzled by what they described as Frieda's "overreaction." As usual, they felt their war of words had cleared the air. They felt more resentful of Frieda's scolding than of their differences.

Comfortability with raised voices and forceful disagreement may be greater for men. Communication experts have observed that even calm communication between males contains a goodly share of one-upsmanship, playful putdowns, and verbal sparring. Wanting things to go smoothly, women are more likely to get rattled when an argument gets rolling. Yet far from necessarily being destructive or even distancing, conversational conflict can indicate mutual comfort. Agreeing that it's OK to disagree, some men find that combat with a friend or co-worker adds spice to their relationship.

When your co-worker can't take the heat—

1. *Steam in private*. Watch where and how you let off steam. If you have conflict-sensitive colleagues, do your dueling privately, not in hallways, at meetings, or in front of outsiders.

2. *Adjust your office thermostat*. Recognize that there are different disagreement styles and adjust if there's a chance you'll be heard as out of control. The temperature is too high if:

- voices are loud enough to reach the next room, even with doors shut
- accusatory language is included, such as:
"Why didn't you . . ."
"You never . . ."
"For once, why couldn't you . . ."
"You wasteful sweat hog . . ."
"You dirty rat . . ."
- faces are fierce. You don't want to resemble Hannibal Lecter from *Silence of the Lambs* or anyone else in the Mass Murderer Hall of Fame.

3. *Tell her it's cool*. She'll feel better if you offer indications that you're not really about to make mincemeat of your office mate. Temperamentally timid people easily misperceive arguments as precursors to physical fighting.

"Chill out, Frieda, we just have to get our disagreement out of our systems."

"If you hear us arguing later, I'm just trying to get Guy to see sense for a change."

I find it difficult to give positive feedback.

Appropriately applied, praise can inspire employees to develop skills and positive attitudes. Complimenting with ease is thus an important communication trait for your managerial repertoire. Though people of both genders can find praising comfortable or an effort, women's greater tendency to focus on creating good feelings makes them more likely to offer appropriate commendation.

Rudolph grew up in a family where good work was expected but never praised. He felt his upbringing helped develop backbone and independence. Applying this credo in his own business, an outdoor clothing outlet, seemed to be backfiring, though. Grace, his bookkeeper, quit because she had become convinced she couldn't do anything right. Rudolph swore he had never once criticized competent Grace. True enough, but according to Grace he had never once extended praise, either. Rudolph couldn't keep expecting his help to live on paychecks alone, lacking the nourishment of positive feedback. Fortunately, his metamorphosis from reluctant reinforcer to proficient praiser didn't take long.

Giving praise when praise is due

1. *Commend yourself for commending others*. If praising isn't your native suit, you may feel awkward when you begin distributing kudos. Understand that even if you've thrived without feedback, some of your employees feel at a loss or even incompetent without it. Grace, for example, had a husband who made a point of a positive mention about her appearance or cooking nearly every day. So Rudolph's silence seemed cold and disapproving

in comparison. When Rudolph tried to woo Grace back by complimenting her ability, he was encouraged to see a smile flicker across her face.

2. *Pour it on.* Commit yourself to complimenting at least one employee or colleague a day. This conservative approach forces you to notice and verbally reward someone in the act of commendable performance, without demanding that you pour it on too thick as you develop a new habit.

3. *Hand it to them—so it's well received.* Effective tribute takes finesse. Keep these tips in mind:

• Compliment as soon as possible after good performance.

"Grace, those forecasts you gave me this morning for next year seem extremely detailed. Thanks."

• Applaud the action more than the actor. Avoid gauche gushing by keeping remarks on the deed, not the doer. In the work environment, acknowledging a job well done leads to other well-done jobs, because your employee learns exactly what actions "score points."

DON'T SAY: "Grace, you're an amazing analyst."
TRY: "Grace, your books are the most orderly I've ever seen."

• Dare to go a step further and encourage future successes.

"I'm glad you took the initiative to audit the branch offices. I can easily see you in a VP position in the region some day. Thanks, Grace."

I don't like to discuss my accomplishments.

Many men have no trouble spitting out ten years of accomplishments after an initial handshake. They also may be highly skilled at one-upsmanship—competitive telling to secure an equal or greater status. But if you're a woman, acknowledging your own accomplishments or what you do better probably smacks of bragging. Since the days when you spent hours skipping rope in the schoolyard, you've known that bragging wins you enemies and disapproval. Where harmony is concerned, you're correct to be cautious about tooting your own horn, since research suggests that assertive people come across as more competent but, alas, less likable.

Yet trying to remain likable in business to the extent of staying silent about your strengths keeps you low on the career ladder. In their pathbreaking studies of women in management, Margaret Hennig and Anne Jardim have shown that women wait to be chosen, unlike men, who often overtly promote themselves. If your reticence to reveal your achievements is holding you back at work, perhaps there is a better way to **B-R-A-G.**

To shed timidity about your triumphs:

Break away from old beliefs.

Old: People will not like me if I talk about myself.

New: Some people won't like me no matter what I do. Although I may be resented by a few, I have the right to move ahead.

Old: If I'm doing a good job, it will be noticed.

New: The speaking wheel gets the grease. I must be a one-person PR firm.

Relate what makes you great. Every career-climbing situation, from a job interview to addressing stockholders when you're chair of the board, involves letting others in on your talents and achievements. Some questions to help you go ahead and give yourself a round of applause:

1. *Will revealing my accomplishments add to the image I'd like in this situation?* Tina, a talented art restorer who stuttered every time she told a prospective client she studied at Harvard University, agreed that to come across as knowledgeable and sophisticated, her degree would help.

2. *Will relating my achievements now help in any career moves for the future?* Even in a social situation, Tina recognized that her top-notch credentials would be remembered for networking, should she ever switch positions.

3. *Will the benefits of bragging outweigh the disadvantages?* The pluses in numbers 1 and 2 were stronger than the chances that where she went to school would alienate someone, she decided.

4. *Am I genuinely proud of what I've achieved, or am I just puffing myself up?* Since Harvard was hardly the kind of school anyone could sail through without hard work, Tina regarded her having graduated with honors as a real distinction.

If you answered "yes" to any of these four questions, you're ready for the next step.

Articulate your new attitude. Some methods to minimize your fear of boasting:

1. *Put the focus more on the work than you.*
Not: "I'm a Harvard grad."
Try: "I got my degree in art history from Harvard and interned at the Museum of Fine Arts."

2. *Learn to throw in your claims to fame without fanfare.*
"That reminds me of my work at Harvard. One of my professors specialized in Courbet."
"In your ad, you mentioned how important good design skills are in this position. I brought some samples of my work you're free to look at."

3. *Avoid mannerisms that undercut your message.* If you gulp, cough, lower your volume, or raise your pitch while mentioning your accomplishments, your listener gets a mixed signal and may question your confidence or credibility. Tina rehearsed her initial introduction to a client while riding to work with a friend. She confided in me, "After a while, talking about what I've done right became as easy as putting myself down."

Go for it. Notice how your effective communication puts you center stage and enhances the chances that good things will come your way. Start to see your ability to share your achievements as another competence. Even better, realize that your insights, talents, and expertise will be helpful to many when you let them in on them.

*I don't work well for bosses
of a certain sex.*

Admitting a preference for a boss of a certain sex is certainly not in vogue at a time when, except for top executive suites, the sex ratio among managers is on the way toward evening out. Over the course of the last generation, rampant prejudice against female managers has abated. In a classic 1965 *Harvard Business Review* article entitled "Are Women Executives People?" 41 percent of men surveyed viewed women bosses unfavorably, and just 27 percent said they'd be comfortable working for a woman. When the same study was conducted again in 1985, only 5 percent of men maintained that women weren't equipped to be bosses. Nevertheless, in the more recent poll, one-half of the male executives and one-fifth of the females confessed discomfort at the prospect of working for a woman.

A feeling of discomfort about working for either sex as a group more likely stems from your beliefs than from differences in your supervisor's style or competence that really matter. Naturally any individual boss can be a bomb, but if you detect the signs of boss bias, it's important to confront it.

After a succession of dictatorial male supervisors, Shanna was delighted that her new manager at the bank was a well-respected older woman, Lillian. But after two weeks of being told what to do at every turn, not to mention Lillian's commentary about her skirts being too short, Shanna sadly watched her dream-boss hopes be shattered. She also worried that some day she'd have to act the same to rise in her career.

How to recognize boss bias

1. *You make judgments about your boss based on gender rather than behavior.*
"She's too distant for a woman."
"I never met a guy so sweet."
Shanna had a right to her disappointment but it would be incorrect to conclude that either all women bosses would be as critical as Lillian or that as a woman she'd have to act that way herself to be successful.

2. *You experience discomfort or a negative attitude before you've given the person a chance.* You're not alone. Both men and women believe that masculine traits and managerial traits are synonymous. Yet people who have had good experiences with opposite-sex bosses and men who have career women in their lives as wives or friends do overcome initial barriers.

3. *You have standards for your boss's behavior based on his or her sex.* For example:
He should have influence in the company, be strong and decisive, focus on getting the job done.
She should be kind, be a mentor, be especially helpful to other women, focus on people getting along.
Don't box your boss in by expecting certain behavior just because of his or her gender. This puts anyone in a bind. People in her department criticized Lillian for not having an open-door policy as did the other women managers in the bank. Having just been promoted, perhaps Lillian needed some time alone to think.
Though Shanna knew she didn't care for aspects of Lillian's style, she also realized that her set of rules called "How a Woman Manager Should Act According to Shanna" need not apply.

Women who work for me won't express their grievances directly.

Fear of criticizing authority figures is common and in many settings reasonable. When you're the one who evaluates performance and hands out rewards, employees worry that pointing out your weak spots can mean trouble for themselves. Female employees and colleagues may inhibit helpful feedback to avoid hurting your feelings, appearing impolite, or being considered overly aggressive. As a result, you remain in the dark about what's going wrong or what could go better.

Stuart, a hospital safety and security director, said he was more content with his male staff members because he'd been burnt by female employees a couple of times. Stuart felt men were more open about criticizing his management style and making suggestions. Apparently two women had been complaining about his "overbearing personality" but never to him. Stuart only found out about their gripes after they left his department. Genuinely eager for constructive feedback, he wondered if he could make it easier for women to offer their complaints to him.

How to get them to give it to you

1. *Ask for it*. Ask frequently for feedback about how things are going. Consider setting up meetings aimed at soliciting employee grievances. Stuart added a "get it off your chest" session to the agenda of his monthly department meetings. In some situations, having staff anonymously complete a form increases candor. "Asking for it" initiations include:

"What do you like and dislike so far about working here?"

"What's one thing you'd like to change about how we work together?"

"I wasn't sure about your reaction to . . ."

"Are you upset about something I did?"

"I overheard someone say our department has problems. What do you think they might be?"

2. *Take it once you get it.* Since it takes courage to criticize a colleague or superior, make every attempt not to act defensive. If your back doesn't go up, you make it more likely that she'll speak up again. Since women may be especially concerned about wounding feelings, offer explicit reassurance that you find constructive input helpful. Even if you can't help your nonverbal response, come out with words of acceptance.

"Thanks for letting me know that . . ."

"I'm glad you spoke up."

"That's important for me to think about."

"I'm surprised that you've been feeling overworked, but glad you finally told me."

3. *Recognize that women and men may dish it out differently.* Gender can affect comfortability with giving negative feedback. Your male co-workers, more concerned with feeling in control, may find directly speaking up more gratifying than holding back. Their critiques may be blunt, especially to other men who they feel will have no trouble taking it. Male managers like Stuart need to appreciate the faint red flags raised by some female employees. In retrospect, for example, Stuart realized that both dissatisfied women had acted withdrawn around him and that he had done most of the talking in their discussions. Given that these women were usually forthcoming with ideas, their passivity pattern could have served as a clue. Other ways women may be letting you know all's not well include:

- avoiding you professionally and/or socially
- not soliciting your input on projects and tasks
- showing obvious preference for consulting with others at your level
- dropping subtle disparaging hints. One of the women remarked to Stuart that the air in the office sometimes seemed thick. Stuart assumed she was talking about poor ventilation. Actually it was Stuart, not the air, which she found oppressive.

I'm not sure the way I shake hands is appropriate.

As brief as it lasts, the business handshake serves as a significant barometer of initiative and self-confidence. Though in business both sexes commonly shake hands upon meeting, from eons ago and even now men have been the shake-happy gender. In his sojourns among different cultures, anthropologist Desmond Morris noted that two-thirds of the handshakes he observed were between men. Men also more frequently than women extend a hand to someone they already know. Traditional etiquette reinforces sexual stereotypes, teaching women not to use a heartier shake than a man and teaching men that it's OK to crunch a man's bones but not a woman's in the process of saying hello. Fortunately, when people judge your handshake harshly, the cures are simple and effective.

In telemarketing time-sharing property in the Bahamas, Paul held a better record than his colleagues. But Alison, his sales manager, noticed a discrepancy between his ability to pull in prospects by phone and his ability to close sales in person. During a role-playing exercise with Paul, Alison was immediately turned off by his almost lifeless handshake. Though his presentation was flawless, the creepiness of his handshake lingered for her and, she suspected, for his potential investors. Though Alison's observation was uncomfortable to hear, Paul felt relieved that the problem was in his hands to solve.

Shape up your handshake
(See if any of these traits put you on shaky ground)

1. *Wimpy*. Your shake is routinely less forceful than that of the person you're greeting (Paul's problem).

New routine: Up the tension in your squeeze and the vigor of your shake.

Men: In your effort not to break a woman's hand, you may be backing off too far from a strong enough greeting. Practice with a female friend to attain a shake of moderate strength.

2. *Slimy*. Your palms sweat a lot, perhaps especially in new social situations.

New routine: Put talc or unscented, greaseless deodorant on your palms for stressful situations or wipe them dry before greeting.

3. *Jerky*. An uneven rhythm in your shake conveys a less than smooth image.

New routine: Practice shaking to the following beat:

Shake / pause / shake / pause

Use a smooth downward stroke, so that your mutual clasp moves four to six inches on the downbeat.

4. *Crushing*. Your shake hurts the other person, especially where there's a King Kong–Fay Wray difference in size.

New routine: Adjust your squeeze to the hand in your hand. Ask someone smaller than you to lend a hand for practice.

Women: Watch out for overcompensating with a bone-crusher. You don't want to play into the too-aggressive stereotype.

Additional pointers on handshaking

- If you sandwich her hand between your hands, you'll come off as dominant.
- If you offer your hand palm up instead of sideways, you'll signal a weaker position.
- If you offer your hand with your fingers stacked up parallel to the floor and match the tension offered by your partner, that's the ideal shake.

An opposite-sex colleague has an embarrassing personal habit.

Most people are sensitive about bringing up sensitive issues, loathe to cause someone embarrassment. This discomfort grows when gender-related concerns come into play, and intensifies even more when the habit belongs to someone higher up in the hierarchy. When boss Billie walks around with her slip showing or supervisor Sam often scratches his crotch when he sits with you, you face a formidable communication challenge. Even as a communication consultant, I'm still trying to get up the nerve to let an executive client of mine know that he should leave the seat down in a unisex restroom. Though it's tempting to avoid the topic and live with your uneasy feeling, you'll both be better off without the embarrassing habit.

Spilling embarrassing news to a co-worker

1. *Pass*. Ask another person to do the telling if he's more comfortable than you with the embarrassing topic or better friends with the offender.

2. *Back door*. Comment on other people who have the bad habit and reveal how you feel about it, never letting on you know she's the guilty one. Or make a comment on the offensive behavior in general. Chances are that the guilty party will become self-conscious, take the hint, and reform.

"It really annoys me when men leave up the seat in a unisex bathroom. It's like they aren't aware of women's presence at all."

"My daughter told me that women have a code word

they use when another woman's slip is showing. What is it, whipped cream? Snow? Blizzard?"

3. *Mime*. Depending on the habit, you can sometimes spur a person's awareness of their need to straighten out by acting out what they need to do yourself. Mary, bothered by her secretary Glen's tendency to return from lunch with crumbs or chocolate smudges on his chin, began checking her face in the mirror in front of him. Add explanatory words if the message doesn't get through.

"I like to make sure my lunch hasn't left mustard or sandwich crumbs behind on my face."

4. *Slide*. State your concern in the form of a suggestion, smoothly and matter-of-factly, as if it were no big deal—even if the stench of his cologne is assaulting your nasal passages. Add a face-saving explanation if you're worried about mortifying the other person. If raising the issue embarrasses you painfully, reward yourself after work for bravery.

"I wish you'd keep your hands off yourself when we talk."

"Since we all use the same restroom, we women would appreciate your remembering to put the seat down before you leave."

"My nose goes ballistic when it's overwhelmed. I'd love it if you came in with less cologne."

Women in my office stop talking when I walk by, and resume when I pass.

Either you're paranoid, they're stunned by the sight of you, or more likely, oops—you've unknowingly walked into a girl-talk zone. Your female co-workers clam up when you appear because they think you wouldn't be interested (How often do you discuss the best place to buy throw pillows?); you would trivialize the topic ("They spent an hour talking about blow-drying hair!"); or you or they would be embarrassed by your presence (Do you really want to hear the details of a chronic yeast infection?). If your appearance dampens discussion, don't take the exclusion personally. Remember that although women can talk politics, policies, and productivity, they may prefer not to when they touch base with friends.

If you could play Tootsie for a day and listen in, here's some of what you'd hear.

Girl talk (Stuff women talk about only with each other)

- details about dates and mates
- how fat they feel
- what would look good with what
- clothes on sale
- frustration with hair
- mothers and mothers-in-law
- tragedy in the news that saddens or disgusts
- cramps and other menstrual problems
- menopausal hot flashes
- new diets and exercise regimens
- in-depth analysis of why so-and-so should dump so-and-so

- rating co-workers' demeanor and attire
- big decisions (getting divorced)
- small decisions (giving up chocolate)
- men—the ones at home
- men—the ones at work (so maybe you're not paranoid)

Zoning out

In one study, 63 percent of women said they *need* same-sex conversations, compared to only 43 percent of men. So if groups of women hush when you show up, respect the purpose of the girl-talk zone and stifle your suspicions.

> If they're talking, keep on walking.
> Don't be a spy—if they appear embarrassed, say good-bye.

I feel left out of sports talk.

If you find yourself in a totally different ballpark than the opposite sex, semantically speaking, you're not alone. Not only do men talk more about sports than women, but sports, more so than hairdos, decorating, or feeding schedules, serve as an important source of terminology for day-to-day business. Even women who are not into sports probably know some fundamentals—referring to a boss as the "coach," to a good effort as a "college try," or to the ultimate goal of business deals as "scoring." In her classic book, *Games Mother Never Taught You*, Betty Lehan Harragan advises women that different corporate cultures and even departments within companies may be influenced by the preferences of the men in charge for, say, baseball over football jargon. She suggests that women spend some time in the stands figuring out what game, linguistically speaking, the powerful ones in an organization are playing.

When sports talk feels like a foreign arena—

1. *Observe from the sidelines.* Whether you're athletically interested or not, pay attention to the lingo used in your business settings. Make note of terms which aren't in your working vocabulary ("over the fence," "down for the count," "birdied"). As if you were learning an expression in another language, try to figure out the particular meaning conveyed by the term. Chances are it's used because it offers connotations ordinary phrases don't. For example, it's more vivid to tell Lisa, "You were a great pinch hitter with the Douglas account" than to say, "Lisa, you were a great help as a temporary replacement in an emergency situation."

2. *Be wary of fumbling*. Because sports are so central to many men's lives, they may conclude you're a grade-D dolt when you know nothing about ice hockey. It's better to pull someone aside after the meeting than to speak up and ask, "The 'Wayne Gretzky of computers'? Who's he?" or say, "Excuse me, some of us don't know what a cross check is." Find a sports coach who will confidentially fill in the blanks of your sports knowledge off the ice, without condescension.

3. *Warm up*. Using language similar to that of clients and colleagues can facilitate close business bonds. Start by incorporating commonly used sports expressions gradually in your business talk. Get comfortable by tossing them around in a familiar field before trying them when at bat in the big leagues. Lisa had no trouble referring to obstacles in the way of deals as "sandtraps" but knew she'd fumble if she tried to use "end runs" or "punting" in talking about investment takeovers. The fellows in her unit loved football, but that was Lisa's least favorite sport.

4. *Play cautiously*. Even if you're a jock, be aware that Monday morning quarterbacking with the guys on the job may still make you feel left out. Some men consider sports a masculine sanctum and they feel a sports-savvy female is acting out of bounds. If you're a rookie at sports talk, like Lisa, they'll roll their eyes in pity or contempt if you ask how the Celtics did over the weekend during the time of year when you should have asked about the Red Sox.

People at work call me "honey" and I hate it.

Your resentment is well-founded, since the use of endearments (sweetie, honey, cutie, doll) in professional relationships correlates with domination. The right to use affectionate terms belongs to those who hold more power or see themselves as more powerful in a situation. Teachers honey pupils, but pupils don't honey back, parents cutie pie kids and not vice versa and so on. You can also observe older adults honeying younger adults, as if they were children. ("I'll help you with that data base, dear," says the fiftyish librarian to the bearded graduate student.) Since maternalism or paternalism, rather than dominance, may be operating here, some recipients of these sweetnesses find them comforting, while others feel condescended to.

In intimate relationships, endearments have a different function. When couples dear each other equally, it's a way of bonding, not belittling.

If "honeys" bother you—

1. *Understand the purpose the endearment serves for your colleague.* Is it an intentional show of power ("Sweetie pie, could you get us some fresh coffee?") or a harmless (to them) way of showing warmth? Then you can make a reasoned judgment about the damage done by the honeys and the consequences of confrontation.

2. *Try one of these strategies for dealing with unwanted "babes," "kittens," and "toots."*

- The echo technique. Repeat the endearment in a tone that says, "I can't believe what I just heard."

"I never knew how fast you were on the word processor, babe."

"Babe?"

Your offender can't help but get the hint. This doesn't mean he'll stop, of course, but now he's aware.

- The give it back technique. Make the endearments reciprocal. You'll feel strange, but it sure will close the power gap. She might feel startled and quit the verbal smooching just to stop you.

"Thanks for getting the report done so promptly, dear."

"No problem, hon."

- Consciousness-raising approach. Try this with a reasonable person who because of an unusual upbringing or an odd habit feels compelled to sprinkle every sentence with sentiment. State your concern and the impact it has on you. You can also offer to help them stop.

"Darling, we're due in John's office at three."

"Ken, when I'm called 'darling' at work, I feel ridiculous and get embarrassed."

"I—er—"

"I know it's just a habit. Is there any way I can help you stop?"

- The sweetie signal. If you get this far, congratulations. Agree that you'll signal nonverbally (hand in the air, a tap of the pen) whenever you hear "honey" or its cousins.

Words for wooing,
not the workplace:

cutie, cutie pie	doll
honey, hon,	sugar
honeybunch	animal names
sweetie, sweetie pie	(kitten, lamb)
darling	sexy
babe, baby	foxy
lover	tootsie

Sexist language used in my organization bothers me.

Henry, a nurse who daily coped with trauma in an inner-city emergency room, found himself waging an internal battle over the way nurses were referred to at his hospital and in his local professional group. Some doctors, administrators, and fellow nurses who should have known better had an automatic link between the word "nurse" and the pronoun "she," although Henry was one of about 93,000 nurses in the United States properly referred to as a "he." When he heard things such as: "Nurses, bring your husbands or boyfriends to the June barbecue," he wanted to explode. Henry wished he knew some way to sound off without seeming either hostile or overly sensitive.

Although we're taught as children to chant, "Sticks and stones may break my bones but names will never hurt me," language can in fact have a serious impact. Studies of children, teenagers, and college students reveal that when a term like "salesman" is used, they think it refers only to men, while a neutral term like "salesperson" evokes either male or female in their minds. Similarly, in a study of high schoolers' career thinking, they showed greater openness to a variety of occupations when gender-neutral terms like "police officer" rather than "policeman" or "policewoman" were used. Here are some strategies to use when you're ready to move to the front lines of the language war.

Combatting sexist language

1. *Gather ammunition*. Isolate specific examples of the usages you consider offensive. Prepare acceptable alternatives so that you can provide solutions. If you think

you might encounter the objection that you're making a big deal out of nothing, get ready to show that breaking the bias habit is a very simple matter. Some sample problems and substitutions:

- The pronoun plight:

DON'T SAY: "Every employee should recheck his withholding status at the personnel office next week."

TRY: "Please recheck your withholding status at the personnel office next week." (use "you" instead of "he")
or
"Employees should check their withholding status at the personnel office next week." (use plural nouns and pronouns) *or*
"Every employee should recheck his or her withholding status at the personnel office next week." (add "or her")

- Typecasting in job titles:

INSTEAD OF:	USE:
mailman	letter carrier
stewardess	flight attendant
spokesman	representative

- Phrasing that assumes or excludes:

INSTEAD OF:	USE:
male nurse	nurse
woman doctor	doctor
nurses and their husbands	nurses and their spouses/families

2. *Choose your arena of battle*. Keep your goal in mind: eliminating offensive language. If you immediately object when you hear sexist language, you run the danger of making the speaker unduly defensive. Consider other means of raising consciousness and producing change:

- writing a memo on the general issue, without pointing a finger at anyone in particular
- inviting in a speaker on sexist language
- posting a list of suggested changes on a bulletin board

Henry decided to post a memo on a bulletin board at the hospital and to write a letter to the editor of the local nurses' association's newsletter.

3. *Fire nonlethal rounds.* Without preaching or scolding, tell the sexist-language offender what could be improved and why.

"Let's remember the male nurses next time and invite wives as well."

"I'd feel more comfortable if you said 'chairperson.' That includes everyone."

Is it better not to open doors and carry stuff for women?

Politeness is always appropriate. If you would open a door, carry a package, or buy a cup of coffee for a man *or* a woman, you're probably engaging in etiquette equality. However, it's important to know when the opposite sex might view your p's-and-q's behavior as offensive. A woman for whom you hold out a chair may resent appearing fragile—and therefore less competent—in a business environment. So don't be shocked if you encounter someone who doesn't respond well to your courtly manners.

Chris, a forty-five-year-old software company vice-president, was raised to, as he put it, "worship women." In fact, most of his women co-workers appreciated his adulation, including one who said he had mastered "chivalry without chauvinism." Chris was miffed when a visiting female executive chided him for volunteering to get the car while asking her, the lone female in the group, to wait inside the restaurant. He needs to figure out—

When politeness is patronizing

Politeness may come across as condescending, invoking the roles of the strong, superior male and the frail, helpless female when—

  • You single her out for special treatment because she's a woman, especially in a situation where the issue of power matters. Fetching the car was fine, but Chris could have asked everyone who wanted to wait indoors to do so.

  • You insist on having your way even when she

objects. The visiting executive told Chris not to bother with the car, but he insisted. In this case, his politeness became a pain.

• You draw attention to a woman's femininity or physical weakness in the course of an ordinary social ritual like walking her to her car. Avoid comments like these:

"You look like you could use a little help."

"I'd never let a woman pick up the check."

"It must be hard for you to carry that huge portfolio around."

Etiquette equality

1. *As much as possible, do for men as you would for women in the workplace.* Open doors for both male and female clients, call a cab for all, treat them both to breakfast.

2. *Do what your mother and father taught you.* Don't inhibit the urge to assist, aid, or add to your colleague's comfort, but be aware of signals that she doesn't appreciate gallantry. Stop being so polite if she—

• acts embarrassed at your efforts

• teases you for your attempts ("I surely couldn't have made it across the street without your holding my arm")

• tells you to cool it ("That's OK—I can do it myself")

3. *If you're not sure how she might respond, ask!*

"May I pick up the check for you?"

"May I take your arm on this busy street?"

"Would you like some help with that suitcase?"

When gallantry gets to you—

Nine out of ten times, his niceness is well meant, not intended as a putdown. So go easy if you need to tell him to tone down.

"Chris, I appreciate your concern about my getting soaked. But there's no need to single me out because I'm a woman."

"Maybe if I were moving to the Arctic Circle, I wouldn't be able to manage my suitcase. But this portfolio case weighs less than a bag of groceries."

If you see Mr. Manners frequently, an educational woman-to-man chat may be in order.

"Larry, these days many businesswomen don't want special treatment. It makes us look less capable than we are. So from now on, let's split the checks and carry our own briefcases, OK?"

A person of the opposite sex at work stares at my body.

No matter what the setting, it is close to impossible to ignore attributes of the opposite sex, or whichever sex appeals to you. The only sure way to interact asexually would be for all of us to walk around inside barrels. This issue especially affects women. According to a Roper Organization poll, at a first meeting 45 percent of American men pay more attention to a woman's figure than to her eyes or smile. Only 16 percent of the women claimed to find a man's physique most compelling at first.

But the invasion of a body watcher in your work space can threaten your poise and your dignity. Charlotte, a sales manager for a clothing store, felt harassed by the store owner's habit of saying hello straight to her chest. This staring behavior, often perpetrated by the higher ranking of two people, can be a way of creating a power imbalance. He exercises his "right" to look you up and down while you are supposed to stand by and be looked at. Besides being annoying, obnoxious ogling interferes with your serious purpose in the organization. During those moments under a gawking eye, you're not a professional but a bunch of body parts. A lascivious leerer deserves a black eye, but of course that wouldn't be businesslike either. Still, there are ways to—

Get back at the body watchers

1. *Avoid a timid response*. Don't avert your eyes, tilt your head, or giggle. That signals that the stares are tolerable.

2. *Avoid exposure if possible*. Situate yourself or your seat to be less visible. Wear your coat or protect yourself with a large portfolio. Charlotte found that her boss acted most normal when she positioned herself behind a pile of clothing that reached the level of her neck.

3. *Avoid the ogler altogether*. As soon as the behavior starts, extinguish it by ending the interaction. Perhaps she'll get the message that she is not your favorite person. This strategy works for brief hallway encounters and informal conversations at work.

4. *Approach the offender head-on*. If you've had enough (and one instance of inappropriateness may be too much), consider these methods for ending the creepy behavior.

- The assume-he's-innocent method. Act as if you're telling him information he probably wasn't aware of.
"I'm sure you don't mean to be offensive, but did you know that you stare at my body when we talk?"
- The assertive statement:
"Jim, I'd appreciate it if you'd speak to me, not my chest."
"Brenda, I'm embarrassed by the way you look at me."
"Connor, do I have purple spots on my blouse or something?"
- Staring contest. Animals determine who's boss by staring each other down. Look at him the way he looks at you. Finally you won't be alone in feeling uncomfortable. And since he's caught off guard, he's likely to break first.

P.S. Drop a copy of this in the offender's mail:

Ogler, wake up.
You're way off base.
Quit looking at my body
And focus on my face.

INDEX